D0758352

THE CULTURE
AND CONTROL
OF EXPERTISE

Recent Titles in
Contributions in Librarianship and Information Science
Series Editor: Paul Wasserman

An Introduction to Online Searching
Tze-chung Li

University Science and Engineering Libraries
Second Edition
Ellis Mount

Environmental Information in Developing Nations: Politics and Policies
Anna da Soledade Vieira

Federal Aid to State Library Agencies: Federal Policy Implementation
David Shavit

Sex Segregation in Librarianship: Demographic and Career Patterns of Academic
Library Administrators
Betty Jo Irvine

Missionaries of the Book: The American Library Profession and the Origins of
United States Cultural Diplomacy
Gary E. Kraske

The Politics of an Emerging Profession: The American Library Association,
1876–1917
Wayne A. Wiegand

Foreign Students in American Library Education: Impact on Home Countries
Maxine K. Rochester

Academic Librarians and Cataloging Networks: Visibility, Quality Control, and
Professional Status
Ruth Hafter

Activism in American Librarianship, 1962–1973
Mary Lee Bundy and Frederick J. Stielow, editors

Librarianship: A Third World Perspective
Rosario Gassol de Horowitz

Pascal Programming for Libraries: Illustrative Examples for Information Specialists
Charles H. Davis, Gerald W. Lundeen, and Debora Shaw

THE CULTURE
AND CONTROL
OF EXPERTISE

Toward a Sociological Understanding
of Librarianship

Michael F. Winter

Contributions in Librarianship and Information Science
Number 61

GREENWOOD PRESS
New York • Westport, Connecticut • London

Library of Congress Cataloging-in-Publication Data

Winter, Michael F.
  The culture and control of expertise.
  (Contributions in librarianship and information
science, ISSN 0084–9243 ; no. 61)
  Bibliography: p.
  Includes index.
  1. Library science—Sociological aspects.
2. Professions—Sociological aspects.   I. Title.
II. Series.
Z665.W78   1988   305.9092   88–174
ISBN: 0–313–25537–7 (lib. bdg. : alk. paper)

British Library Cataloguing in Publication Data is available.

Library of Congress Catalog Card Number: 88–174
ISBN: 0–313–25537–7
ISSN: 0084–9243

First published in 1988

Greenwood Press, Inc.
88 Post Road West, Westport, Connecticut   06881

Printed in the United States of America

The paper used in this book complies with the
Permanent Paper Standard issued by the National
Information Standards Organization (Z39.48–1984).

10 9 8 7 6 5 4 3 2 1

10–30–89

For Ellen, Chris, and for Bill and Dot

Contents

Figures   xi

Preface   xiii

1   The Rise of the Modern Professions   1

2   Early Efforts: The Emergence of the Trait Theory   21

3   Differentiation and Contrast: Functionalist and
    Occupational Control Theories of the Professions   39

4   The Keepers of the Keys: Librarianship as Occupational
    Control   57

5   The Social Context of Control: The Social Background, the
    Schools, and the Association   77

6   The Trick Question: Thinking Through the Occupation/
    Profession Debate   97

7   Search for a New Model: An Exploration   115

8   Librarianship as an Occupation: Suggestions for Research   129

    Bibliographical Essay   145

    Index   149

Figures

3–1 Comparison of Trait and Functionalist Models   43

4–1 Interaction of Normative and Structural Foundations   61

5–1 Background Factors, Occupational Institutions, and Work Arrangements   78

7–1 Aspects of Freedom in Professional Work   120

7–2 General Comparison of Models   124

7–3 Areas of Convergence   125

Preface

Scholars have larger, perhaps more interesting, as well as smaller and more manageable goals. The big goals are often overly ambitious, perhaps even grandiose, but they nevertheless perform the essential function of setting a framework for thinking and writing. They energize and stimulate. In writing this volume, I frankly hope to change the way librarians think about their work, and indirectly the way they work. This challenges some dominant modes of thinking that have been around for some time, and certainly qualifies as a grand aim. The lesser, but perhaps more attainable, purpose of this book is to show how the sociological study of professions and occupations can be used to understand librarianship. Its subject and its method are both theoretical and interpretive.

This work grew out of a long-standing interest in the social theory of industrial society, the study of professions and occupations, and the nature and development of librarianship. All three of these are intimately related and are discussed at some length in Chapter 1, which sets the stage for the rest of the book. Chapter 2 critically examines the first systematic attempt at a theory of professions—what I call the trait theory—and shows how it might be applied to librarianship. Chapter 3 presents the functionalist view of professions, associated with Talcott Parsons and others, but its real business is to show how the contemporary sociological concern with occupational control emerged as a critical response to both the trait theory and the functionalist approach to professions. In Chapter 4 the occupational control approach is discussed further and applied in detail to librarianship. Chapter 5 examines the wider social context that is involved in controlling work, and situates librarianship in this context.

This book also grew partly from a sense of disquiet about librarians' and library educators' own understandings of librarianship. Far too much literature, I came to feel as I read more and more of it, dealt with the old question ''Is librarianship a profession?'' in too narrow and too simple a fashion, and far too little with the questions of professionalism and professionalization in a broader sociological context. Theories of professions and occupations, in other words,

had become scorecards for quick rating and sorting; somehow their larger significance had been lost. This, too, is part of the background of the sociological
discussions of the first five chapters. Chapter 6 confronts this situation directly
and offers a critical view of the occupation/profession debate, urging that we
abandon it, at least in its traditional terms. Chapter 7 tries to define what is
living and what is dead in the study of the professions and proposes a tentative
synthesis as a framework for further thought. In Chapter 8 I hope to capture
some of the richness of the sociological study of work and to make suggestions
for further research, in this case research on librarianship as an occupation. This
ending note is quite intentional, for I wish to suggest that there is an important
sense in which the study of an occupation is far richer and more suggestive than
the traditional concern with achieving the status of something we think of as a
"true" profession, whatever that may be.

I have imposed on so many people that I cannot possibly hope to thank them
all. Thanks are due first to Paul Wasserman for suggesting the project and helping
to shape it; and to Mary Sive, a most conscientious and helpful editor at Greenwood Press. Mary Niles Maack, Patrick Wilson, Pauline Wilson, James S.
Dowling, D. W. Krummel, and Edwin M. Lemert read earlier versions of this
work and made excellent criticisms. Though I did not always follow their suggestions, I benefited greatly from their insights, as I have also benefited from
many discussions with Marcia Pankake. Virginia Short helped arrange my work
schedule to allow some of the peace and quiet necessary for research and writing.
The Librarians Association of the University of California gave me a generous
grant to defray some of the costs of research and publication. I am also indebted
to Gennie Bostock for her indexing experience and expertise.

My greatest debt, however, is to Ellen R. Robert, who critically read and
examined the manuscript in its entirety, and made so many useful suggestions
for changes and revisions that I have now lost track of them all. Her knowledge
and industry have helped me more than I can say.

THE CULTURE
AND CONTROL
OF EXPERTISE

1

The Rise of the Modern Professions

THE NINETEENTH-CENTURY BACKGROUND

In the nineteenth century the great movements of industrialization in Europe and the United States brought vast changes in economic, social, and cultural life. These changes were made possible in part by rapid advances in scientific and technical knowledge, including the invention of the steam engine, the printing press, and other means to increase productivity. But the new sciences and technologies were more than the necessary conditions of industrialization, for they quickly became enmeshed in the factory system of production and its emerging social structure. With this development came a very striking increase in the number and types of occupations found in typical industrial societies when compared with the older societies they were so quickly replacing. In the period between 1870 and 1930 in the United States, for example, there was a dramatic increase in the number of new occupations, as well as an increase in the number of professions considered as a proportion of the total reported by the Bureau of the Census.[1]

Thus what we call professional occupations were, like most contemporary occupations, products of the sudden increase of complexity in the division of labor in the early and middle industrial periods. The change was not only quantitative, for it was not merely a question of an increase in numbers of occupations. It was also a dramatic change of quality, and marked the emergence of a fundamentally new type of social organization. In preindustrial societies occupational structure is a relatively straightforward reflection of the basic social roles of age, sex, and caste or class membership, and because these roles are limited in number, there are relatively few occupations and very little specialization. The industrial period made the occupational structure so much more complex that it produced a fundamentally different type of society characterized by a vast web of interdependent specializations.

In a period of such rapid and dramatic change, many traditional ties were loosened and only later reestablished. The professions, for example—with the exception of the clergy—lost for a time their old exclusive connection with the university, though they regained it toward the end of the nineteenth and the beginning of the twentieth centuries. The reason for this is that the universities remained for a considerable period dominated by older theological interests and failed, until well into the nineteenth century, to represent the newer approaches to learning. By that time, of course, all of the older professions had themselves become thoroughly transformed by the rise of industrial society, and found themselves suddenly in competition with many new occupational groups.[2]

At the same time that the applied versions of the natural sciences were stimulating industrial growth with useful inventions, a need arose for new approaches to the social and human problems that these changes brought about. Thus part of the task of the early social theorists of the period, such as Saint-Simon, Comte, and Spencer, was to describe and attempt to explain how the new type of society functioned, to stress the role that the natural sciences played in all of this, and to begin the work of understanding how human social life had changed in response to it. Sociology in particular, and to a lesser degree political science, economics, and education, were thus the intellectual offspring of industrialization. One of the great problems for the early social sciences was that of understanding the very complex occupational structure of the time.[3]

Like the natural sciences, the role of the social sciences was practical as well as theoretical. Besides trying to understand how the new society functioned, the social sciences provided practical perspectives in the form of "scientific management," "industrial psychology," "social welfare administration," and related areas. Each in somewhat different ways inherited the task of keeping the industrial machinery functioning smoothly: in the first instance by reducing production to a process of calculation, in the second by reducing stress and strain in the workplace, and in the third by looking after problems in private life. Most of this came somewhat later than the early theoretical work of Comte and Spencer, as the scientific applications had followed the earlier theoretical discoveries in chemistry, physics, and the study of electricity. Naturally a considerable part of the occupational increase was represented by newer forms of work in these areas, and the occupational landscape was peopled with new types of service workers. Indeed, writers too numerous to mention have made strong arguments for the claim that the height of the industrial period was also the beginning of the contemporary service-dominated economy. In any case, what is important for present purposes is to note that it is primarily this group of workers that makes up the newer professional occupations.

LIBRARIANSHIP AND THE EMERGENCE OF THE INFORMATION FIELDS

Of course, librarians had existed from the earliest of historic times, much as had doctors, jurists, and priests, though evidence suggests that medicine is probably the oldest of the professions.[4] But although the need for books and other forms of recorded knowledge far predates the industrial revolution, librarians, along with archivists, publishers, and other information-treating occupations, did not begin to show a distinctively modern shape until the late nineteenth and early twentieth centuries. Librarianship's first training school, its first university school, and its first professional associations and licensing procedures all date from the last quarter of the nineteenth century. And while the pursuit of librarianship as a full-time occupation started at least in the eighteenth century, the development of a formal code of ethics did not occur until the late 1930s.[5]

Archives management and information science were slower to develop associations (1933 and 1937, respectively), and although information science now has a number of university programs in force, these developed much later than the library schools. Archival work still remains more or less outside the formal university curriculum, and the field of publishing, really a business specialty, is only beginning to penetrate it. And while information science as a modern discipline may be dated from about the same period as library science, a group of practitioners identifying themselves as such did not really emerge until the period between World Wars I and II, when the great potential of microforms and automation began to be realized in the storage and retrieval of information.

Like other relatively new fields, the information occupations emerged as a result of the increase of complexity in the division of labor, and a parallel increase in the quantity and complexity of the knowledge and available information that are used in typical occupational routines.[6] And like other occupational groups, librarians and other information specialists have found that their work increasingly requires the acquisition of advanced intellectual skills and a mastery of theoretical principles. In these cases the complexity of the occupational structure promotes the need for formal educational programs to train new groups of workers, stimulating newer occupational groups to seek university affiliation.

The relation between the division of labor and the increasing amounts of knowledge is at the heart of the social process we try to pinpoint when we speak of the rise of the modern professions, and it has a special relevance to the development of the information professions. As the number of occupations increases, the total amount of social knowledge that forms the basis of each occupation's activities also increases. Thus each occupation helps to define a new body of specialized knowledge and information, or at the very least a new body of lore, skills, and approaches to work. An occupation is a kind of a cultural world unto itself, and an important part of its constitution is the intellectual capital it draws on to perform its routines. This intellectual capital is referred to as the "knowledge base" of an occupation, understanding *knowledge* in a relatively loose rather than a rigorously logical or philosophical way. Use of the term *knowledge base* does not make an implicit claim that the knowledge used in doing a certain job is somehow better, truer, or more uplifting than any other kind, but only that it is essential to doing that type of work.

At the same time that these specialized bodies of knowledge were growing as a response to changes in the division of labor, there was a parallel growth in the general stock of commonsense knowledge, as parts of specialized fields gradually spill over into the intellectual repertoire of educated people. What starts out as esoteric, known only to practitioners and appearing mysterious to others, in many cases finds its way into the broader culture. But there almost always remains a core of knowledge that resists such diffusion, and it needs to be mastered by anyone who hopes to practice a given occupation. Thus, while almost no one except librarians a century ago knew anything about classification systems, today most educated Americans know that the Dewey and Library of Congress schemes of book classification are among the most common systems used in modern libraries, and most educated people have at least some idea of how to use them. By the same token, however, most educated persons know very little about automation in libraries, collection development, the organizational characteristics of technical report literature, citation analysis, or any number of other areas in contemporary librarianship. Similar examples could be cited from many occupations, including medicine, nursing, law, accounting, architecture, engineering, and others.

From the specialist's point of view, the management of each occupation's knowledge base is part of the work in performing that occupation, and an initial mastery of that knowledge is a minimal condition for entry into the occupational group. But notice that the question of general access to the total of social knowledge represented by occupational growth is a completely different matter; even specialized intellectual workers could not hope to master such vast growth and still maintain a mastery of their own fields. The need for access to the total of shared knowledge really calls for a separate occupation, or more exactly, a separate cluster of occupations, and these are the information fields: librarianship, information science, archives management, publishing, and other areas of work in what Patrick Wilson calls the "bibliographic sector."[7]

THE EXPANDING SOCIAL BASE OF INFORMATION

From a technological point of view, the expansion of knowledge and information, originally promised by the invention of movable-type printing and later realized by the development of mass production techniques, releases vast amounts of knowledge, information, and factual data for consumption.[8] In addition to the technical knowledge of occupational routines, it includes the wide range of practical knowledge used by ordinary people in everyday life, and the pure knowledge of many different branches of scholarship. This aspect of the development of industrial society became so prominent in the early years of the twentieth century that the production and dissemination of information became a partly autonomous site of socioeconomic activity—virtually a separate sector with distinct mechanisms of operation. The key dynamic is the emergence of an immense sector of service, of which the information sector is a smaller part.

Whether or not this means a complete qualitative change to an entirely new type of society, as is sometimes argued, is not for us to decide.[9] From our point of view, it is not really the debate about the postindustrial society that matters, or even the question of the role of the printing process in the production and dissemination of knowledge; what we focus on specifically is the application of modern scientific management techniques to knowledge and information production. The press, after all, is really only the technological instrument that served as the fulcrum for the basic change, which was a revolution in the organization of production and distribution; and the same is true of other inventions. Technological advances permitted a new type of almost purely rationalistic, austerely functional production: mass production, assembly line organization, and a progressively increasing specialization of tasks. The scientific management of the printing and publishing process enables the expanding information base created by the rise of the new occupations to be recorded, distributed, and stored in huge quantities. Without this new type of socioeconomic organization, the printing process would have stayed for much longer at the preindustrial craft level, producing expensive materials totally unsuited for mass distribution and consumption.[10]

USING METASCIENCE: THE ORGANIZATION OF KNOWLEDGE RECORDS

Librarianship was the first of the information-handling occupations to confront the need for new ways of classifying and organizing the recorded forms of this new knowledge. In terms of professionalization, librarianship provides a prototypical information occupation.

By the late nineteenth century it was clear, especially in the United States and Great Britain, that the older bibliophilic model of the scholar learned in philosophy, natural science, and philology would not meet the newer occupational demands, even if a need remained for the older type. Special training in organizational problems was required. It was time for the recognition, in Abraham Kaplan's words, of the need for personnel specialized in the "metasciences"—disciplines that did not hold traditional liberal arts subjects as their main concerns. What was needed was a group of disciplines whose subject would be organization of knowledge itself.[11]

Classification, Indexing, and Bodies of Literature

Strictly speaking, librarianship deals with records of knowledge, and this means that the phrase "organization of knowledge" is by itself too broad. What is organized is the output of records. For our purposes, the organization of knowledge records has three basic aspects. First, the knowledge represented in the records is classified, or arranged according to some conceptual scheme. This is primarily a cognitive operation, an attempt at intellectual organization similar to the scientific classification schemes used for biological organisms or elements, and to philosophical schemes for organizing concepts. In this sense, bibliographic classification is analogous to the Linnean classification, the periodic table, and Francis Bacon's outline of knowledge. Second, there are systems for storing and retrieving records, generally called indexing systems. While classification is an ancient intellectual activity, the development of practical indexing systems is relatively new. Third, there are various bodies of literature that have their own informal organization and display various formal characteristics.

Classification and indexing are meant to tame the wilderness of informally organized bodies of literature, but naturally this happens with varying degrees of success. The difference between the three aspects of knowledge organization in librarianship is really one of emphasis; in real life librarians face the buzzing confusion of all three. They must simultaneously attempt to discern the outlines of knowledge in general; they must develop strategies for finding specific items; and they must recognize that in many cases the actual organization of the body of literature they are searching will elude attempts to classify and index it. In this interaction and combination of different types of intellectual organization, they must find a way; and this is at the center of librarianship's metascientific impulse.

Of course, the organizational dimensions of classification, indexing, and bodies of literature are also the proper domains of occupations other than librarianship. That is clear from Wilson's discussion of the bibliographic sector, which includes "engineers, technicians, librarians, information scientists, indexers, classifications specialists, and documentation workers."[12] Though this book cannot provide an exhaustive definition of the library field, we do need nonetheless to call attention to the way in which librarians differ from these other types of information workers. The library profession is that point in the bibliographic sector where all these aspects of organization are mastered in order to put users in touch with the records that contain the knowledge or information they seek. To some degree, this function is shared with workers who are not necessarily called librarians, just as those workers who *are* called librarians sometimes carry out functions allotted to others. But this is a question of organizational and practical emphasis. Mediating between the user and the public record of knowledge is the special province of the librarian, and it is accomplished by the use of a certain type of metascience.

THE NATURE OF METASCIENCE

Abraham Kaplan's observation that the increase in knowledge production calls for librarians to pay special attention to problems of intellectual organization merits attention. It is the intellectual reflection of a very fundamental social change. Among the established disciplines, philosophy (especially logic and metaphysics), linguistics and philology, and certain types of mathematics may all be said to provide a metascientific perspective, but only in a very theoretical way. Among the newer fields, computer science and informatics are equally obvious examples. Kaplan's idea is particularly suggestive for the older disciplines, which are often barely recognized as part of the knowledge base underlying librarianship as a field of study and practice.

Why is the metascientific impulse so important to us today? One reason is that periods of rapid growth in knowledge tend to cause a great deal of intellectual confusion, just as periods of rapid social change generally cause difficulties of adjustment in identity, group membership, and cultural assimilation. "Metascience," in its most general meaning, is the attempt to study science, and by "science," of course, we mean the entire field of human inquiry. The growth of knowledge becomes so bewildering that it calls for new disciplines whose subjects are organizational rather than substantive—oriented to form rather than content. The impulse behind it is to provide some sense of the structure of knowledge as a whole, and the dream behind it is to provide a set of concepts that would actually bring the various fields together in a kind of master science.[13]

Most of the older liberal arts disciplines have already been significantly affected by the emergence of metascience. Philosophy, for example, has become so specialized as to be virtually hermetic and impenetrable to outsiders, but it has strong metascientific tendencies that have already had considerable influence on librarianship. If we see logic as a discipline that looks for underlying sets of relationships among concepts and propositions and derives sets of rules for combining them, we can see that this can be done for any set of concepts and propositions. Linguistics, where much of the structuralist impulse originated, is a similar organizational tool when applied to forms of discourse, natural and artificial. Insofar as thought is embodied in language, philosophy and linguistics overlap, but this is really only what we expect anyway when we begin to follow the metascientific thread. And linguistics crosses many disciplinary lines, including mathematics, biology, psychology, history, and sociology.

But it may be mathematics, among the traditional liberal arts fields, that has the strongest potential for metascientific understanding. Of all fields, it seems the least dependent on content and is clearly very closely allied to logic at this point. Bertrand Russell joked about mathematics being the field in which we never know what we are talking about. For metascience, this is not a joke but a straight description of its major concern: not with things, but with the forms of things in their various arrangements. The metascientific strains in mathematics and philosophy meet in the field of algebraic logic, in the idea of deriving rules for pure combinations. As we all now know, online searchers apply this general metascientific idea in the formulas for computer searching, even though this is rarely explicit in the act of searching.

LIBRARIANSHIP AS APPLIED METASCIENCE

The examples above illustrate a general point: many, perhaps all, fields of knowledge have a metascientific aspect that can be used as an ordering device or rough scheme of organization. Furthermore, they have acquired this organizational tendency as knowledge advanced to the point where it became clear that new methods were needed to keep track of it. In this is an essential clue to understanding the form of metascientific organization involved in librarianship. For it, too, is a response to the need for organizational means to control and classify the ever increasing pool of knowledge.

In this respect librarianship has an important link with philosophy, a field that makes a strong theoretical contribution to organizational problems. Systems of document classification, for example, are usually based on broad logical assumptions regarding the structure of classes and their interrelationships. The traditional opposition between deduction of particular propositions from general ones, and the establishment of valid empirical generalizations through induction, for example, is reflected in the difference between deductive classification schemes and faceted ones. More recently a third alternative, not precisely conforming to the distinction, represented by the Classification Research Group, argues for ideally flexible systems that pragmatically follow the development of new disciplines and the emergence of interdisciplinary fields.[14] This alternative follows, in effect, the pragmatist rejection of formal logic initiated by John Dewey, and rests tacitly on the idea of an instrumental or experimental logic. It also follows the general contemporary tendency to reject the systematic dimension of classification schemes as overly "metaphysical" in favor of the pragmatic tool. At the moment the matter seems to rest here, but there is no reason why further consideration of developments in logic might not suggest entirely new forms of classification. If earlier theorists looked to Bacon, Russell, and Whitehead, or to pragmatism, contemporary and future classification theorists may turn to a whole series of developments in contemporary logic for new inspiration. And, of course, they might also look to these developments for new ideas in organizing access to online systems, as an earlier generation looked to Boolean algebra for inspiration in searching bibliographic data bases.

The clue for librarianship is that its knowledge base is a form of applied metascience. It is the study of how the universe of published records of knowledge is organized. It bears a certain resemblance to the more theoretical metascientific viewpoints of philosophy, linguistics, and mathematical logic, in that it looks at form in preference to content. But it differs in that its concern with form is not primarily theoretical, except insofar as the purer branches of the field develop in that direction. Where philosophy, linguistics, and mathematics may cultivate a sense of form for its own sake, or where literary criticism may explore the idea of structure as represented in texts in a pure form, librarianship uses the idea of form as a key to provide access to the documents represented in the fields. Librarianship uses form for a practical purpose: to enable users to better find their way from the formal properties of documents to the contents they seek.

The theoretical connection between metascience in philosophy and librarianship is complemented by the practical difficulties that ordinary people experience in finding information. The complexity of contemporary industrial society presents acute problems for routine functioning, and many of these center on the organization, storage, retrieval, and dissemination of information. For Ortega y Gasset, this is the central problem of the modern librarian, as distinguished from the older "keepers" of books and manuscripts, whose functions are closer to preservation than organization.[15] The ideology of preservation, one might say, has partly given way to the ideologies of management and control. Naturally Ortega's insight needs to be broadened a bit to include all of the occupations of the bibliographic sector—he was writing before information science had emerged as a separate discipline, to say nothing of publishing, documentation, and other fields—but what he says still generally holds true. Today, the problems of records preservation are extremely important, but they are nonetheless interpreted in a wider context of managing and controlling documents. Preservation, except in the curatorial functions of special collections, is not an end in itself. This is, of course, an enormous change, representing a decisive break with centuries of librarianship.

It is not accidental that this change from preservation to metascientific management of knowledge records comes along with very fundamental changes in social organization: intellectual and social organization reflect one another, even if they follow different development patterns. The extraordinary growth of knowledge that provided the impetus for the development of modern librarianship, and that so decisively affected all the modern professions, is thus only a part of the story. The other part comes from the rise of new forms of social organization, particularly industrial bureaucracy.

BUREAUCRACY, ANOMIE, AND DISENCHANTMENT

Increasing complexity has become the dominant theme: more occupations, more specialized knowledge supporting them, and more need for coordination in order to increase bibliographic control. Although it sounds as if the coordination required were mainly of the intellectual type, this is only partly true. The need for coordination exists not only at the level of knowledge and information, but, even more basically, at all levels of social and economic organization. Or, said another way, types of specialized social activity need to be coordinated, just as types or provinces of knowledge need to be coordinated by metascience.

The most distinctive type of general social coordination in our time is bureaucratic organization. Unfortunately, bureaucracy does more than coordinate; it is also a major form of social domination. The complexity of industrial and postindustrial society is based on extreme specialization, and bureaucratic organization reflects this, relying on fixed jurisdiction, specialized training of officials, and specialized files recording official versions of standards. Perhaps inherent in specialization itself is a tendency toward fragmentation, which invites powerful parties to subordinate all the different specialties into a hierarchy, with themselves, naturally, at the top of the pyramid. Because bureaucratic organization is so ubiquitous, it affects all aspects of social life. The combination of ubiquity and power tends to make people feel a general loss of freedom, and also a loss of meaning—particularly in work—that cannot be entirely offset by a rising standard of living.

Two theorists of industrial society are of particular importance here: Max Weber and Emile Durkheim. Each in a different way tried to explain the maintenance of social order where older ties were loosened by the advancement of specialization. Both saw that social order was maintained by new types of social control. Durkheim was among the first to see that industrial society had absorbed us into a great, functionally differentiated organism of economic production. Weber saw that the transformation of traditional communities, with their unique local customs and color and flavor, into impersonal mass organizations was accompanied by the emergence of new types of power and prestige. How was social order to be maintained in a social structure that increasingly loosened ties with older forms of local organization? In their absence, what forces would channel human energy so that basic social functions could be fulfilled? Criticizing the limitations of orthodox Marxism, Weber maintained that the "means of production" were supplemented by the "means of administration" and the "means of legitimate violence," by which he meant the authorized powers of the new nation-states. And the means of administration were concentrated, not merely in the hands of managerial and entrepreneurial capitalists, but in positions that controlled the state bureaucracies.[16]

Durkheim and Weber were concerned not only with technical problems of social control, but just as much with the human reaction to them. For if industrial society produced vast amounts of wealth and powerful bureaucracies to control and distribute them, it did far less for the human feelings of alienation that it also produced. In Durkheim's words, the outstanding moral characteristic of modern society is "anomie," which he coined to refer to the pervasive "normlessness" or moral confusion that exists in modern industrial societies. We have little problem with devising efficient means to produce goods or disseminate services, but we have great problems achieving moral consensus. The source of anomie lies in the fact that the individual, and the society as a whole, are cut loose from the earlier traditional consensus about what is right and what is wrong.

For Weber, the stress is somewhat different, but the general problematic is much the same, and he coined the term "disenchantment" to refer to the fact that industrial society had extended the rational domination of nature so thoroughly that it had undermined the older sense of meaning. Industrial society, with its great complexity, had solved many practical problems, but it had, in Weber's view, created a problem of vast proportions, for it removed the ancient sense of belonging to the universe.

While Durkheim's idea of anomie stressed the problem of achieving moral consensus in a world dominated by individual achievement and entrepreneurship, Weber's idea of disenchantment referred to the more general fact that industrialization, with its narrow model of "means—ends" rationality, had stripped the world of its depth and mystery. The advance of this type of rationality dissolves the hold of religion, myth, and philosophy; we come to see ourselves primarily in functional, economic terms—how much profit there is in a certain enterprise. Science and society both collaborate in dispersing the older kinds of belief in purpose and meaning. A poem by William Butler Yeats expresses Weber's idea perfectly (although unintentionally):

> The woods of arcady are dead
> And over is their antique joy,
> Of old the world on dreaming fed
> Grey truth is now her painted toy.[17]

The opposition here between preindustrial tradition and modern rationality is captured by Yeats in the distinction between the images of dark forests, dreams, and antiquity—all traditional symbols of the mythical, the religious, and the unrational—and the flat image of truth as the pursuit of useful facts. Now this characterization of the modern temper as meanly and one-sidedly rationalistic—even childish, as the last word of the poem suggests—is not entirely fair. Surely good scientific research, pure and applied, with its creative excitement and its respect for the unknown, cannot be dismissed so easily. But Yeats does not really have this aspect of scientific rationality in mind; he is thinking much more of the stultifying routine of industrial mechanization, with its relentless profit-and-loss orientation, and its indifference to the spontaneous, the beautiful, and the magical. And, of course, in this he is only echoing the discoveries of the major social theorists. Like Durkheim and Weber, the poet expresses what many have felt.

While Durkheim and Weber were, like Yeats, concerned with the human response to modernity, they were also very much concerned with the analysis of the kind of social organization represented by modern industrialism. For Durkheim the main principle of organization is in the division of labor; for Weber in the formal structure of bureaucracy.[18] The complexity of the division of labor and the mechanism of bureaucratic organization remain two of the principal structural features of contemporary society; between them they constitute the major outlines of the social system.

FREEDOM AND ORGANIZATION

As is often the case in periods of decisive social change, these developments (anomie and disenchantment) were not without their irony. Durkheim had noticed that in certain ways the coming of industrial society meant freedom from older forms of constraint. Indeed, with its bewildering array of occupations, its technological advances, and the concentration of material and intellectual resources in the growing urban centers, industrial society actively encouraged the development of individualism. It provided unsuspected opportunities for amassing wealth and for social and geographic mobility, and it came equipped with an ideology of individual achievement. And yet at the same time that industrial society genuinely liberated individuals from the remains of feudal social organization, it quickly subjected them to its own harsh form of discipline. Max Weber, in an image of striking bitterness reflecting the depth of his pessimism, called it "the iron cage." Socioeconomic complexity requires a parallel complexity of social organization, and this in turn brings formal coordination, hierarchical arrangement, or, to use another of Weber's terms, "rationalization." The key to this use of the term *rational* is the idea that everything is subjected to the needs of efficient production: means are ruthlessly adjusted to ends in the pursuit of profit and material gain. By individualizing persons as workers, by stressing the uniqueness of each occupation's contribution to our social and economic welfare, advanced industrial society had nurtured within itself a counterthrust: the more concerned we are with our individuality and our personal achievements, the less likely we are to like being subjected to bureaucratic routines. And yet the more individuated we become, the greater is the need for authoritative mechanisms of social order to coordinate social action.

We can see in this brief reconstruction of the value crisis of mature industrial society that it involves not only our overall sense of meaning and purpose in life, but also our sense of freedom. In a very interesting way, freedom and meaning turn out to be closely related in this development. The freedom that came with industrialization and the growth of the occupational structure was mainly a freedom from certain types of interference: the interference of custom, tradition, and inherited authority. At about this point in our history emerges a new ideal of individual freedom, sometimes called "negative freedom" by philosophers.[19] It is "negative" because it refuses to specify any positive values to legitimate human action; it only asserts that we should be free from outside interference. Certainly "negative freedom" is extremely important as a contemporary value; among other things, the entire history of liberalism, including the concern with intellectual freedom so important to librarianship, is incomprehensible without it. However important or valuable it may be, it has one very crucial drawback: precisely because it defines freedom negatively, it provides the individual with no sense of purpose other than conscience. Thus, on the philosophical level, negative freedom cuts us off from our value traditions just as the socioeconomic character of industrialism cuts us off from older social life. Thus this new concept of freedom contributes to the general sense of confusion that is behind anomie and disenchantment.

PROFESSIONALIZATION AS RESPONSE TO BUREAUCRACY

Against this extended background of bureaucratization the smaller drama of professionalization, originally played out in medicine, law, university teaching, and the clergy, but later enveloping other occupations, achieves its sharpest resolution. Professionalization, in other words, is one (rather effective) way in which middle-class occupations can resist the encroachment of bureaucratic authority, counteract the moral drift of anomie, and try to protect the values threatened by industrialization.[20] What is at stake here is the attempt by occupational groups to become independent work organizations, to have their own culture, their own mechanisms of control, to regulate their own work, and to use work as one way of making sense of the world. Although Durkheim had not foreseen precisely this, he predicted the formation of guildlike organizations serving as moral communities—buffer zones against the functional anonymity of the modern industrial division of labor.[21] Thus the importance of the professional association, licensing procedures and ethics codes, formal training programs, legitimate monopolies over bodies of knowledge, service orientation, and community recognition.[22] All these legitimate the professional's freedom and protect it, enabling the practitioner to respond to external pressure without submitting to control of outside agents. They also provide a sense of social cohesion founded on occupational goals and values, and encourage the formation of a specifically professionalized personal identity. Professional practice, in this sense, is incompatible with the bureaucratic discipline of the industrial organization, where sharp distinctions between intellectual and manual labor, conception, execution, and the like work to prevent the development of an occupational identity. The "outside influence" noted above is not limited to external authority, but includes the threat of competition from other, allegedly nonlegitimate practitioners. In this light also we can see that the assumption that the service orientation of professional life, rooted in "the pursuit of science and liberal learning," contrasts in a marked way with the rationalizing profit orientation of business.[23]

In terms of a social theory of contemporary industrial society, we can say that professionalization, and generally the impulse to professionalize work, have two very broad dimensions. On the one hand, individuals look to them as ways of meeting the challenges of anomie and disenchantment—as one way of dealing with very general problems of values in human life. But also, and more specifically, professionalization is a way of dealing with the more immediate challenges of bureaucratic authority, in the everyday sense of fighting off the attempts of business to invade spheres of professional practice in hopes of exploiting their potential for profit. This is why the point about the service orientation is important, and should not be dismissed cynically, as it often is. However lucrative certain types of professional service might be, the very notion of service is fundamentally different from, and opposed to, the notion of subjecting the delivery of services to the rationalizing techniques of the profit orientation. This is the crucial distinction, and not the fact that some professionals make more money than others.

PROFESSIONALISM AND BUREAUCRACY: A COMPLEX OPPOSITION

Nonetheless, the relationship between the professions and bureaucratic organization is not one of simple opposition, even though it is sometimes described in that way. The reason is that in certain respects professionalism and bureaucracy are products of the same set of socioeconomic developments. Thus, while it is true that professionals often resist organizational authority, especially when it is perceived as originating outside the occupation, professional services, and often the most efficient means for delivering them, are almost impossible without the economic and technological developments of industrialism, and the bureaucratic organization that arises to regulate them. Also, the older distinction between the independent and the organizationally affiliated professional is much less clear than it used to be, and may be disappearing fast. Very few professionals altogether escape the bureaucratic situation and its effect on work.

Empirical research on bureaucracy and its effect on professional work also leads us to be skeptical of any attempts to portray the relationship between the two as one of simple opposition. The evidence indicates something more complex. It has been shown, for example, that a moderate level of bureaucratization is positively rather than negatively correlated with relatively high levels of professional autonomy. This means that professionals working in complex, highly structured organizations experience, if anything, more freedom in their work than those who work in traditional solo practice arrangements. Perhaps this is because such organizations offer more resources and more support, and thus provide new opportunities for exercising professional expertise. The solo practitioner of days past has, if anything, only the freedom to work at a relatively lower level of complexity. Thus our intuition that professionalism should correlate exclusively with low levels of bureaucratization turns out to be incorrect.[24] Furthermore, as Hall reported a number of years ago, the correlation between professionalism and bureaucratic organization appears to hold for virtually all dimensions of professionalization.[25] What this evidence suggests is that the cause of professionalism, at least up to a point, is enhanced and not inhibited by bureaucracy.

The general point seems to hold quite well for libraries, where it has been found that professionalization is positively correlated with increases in the size of a library organization's administrative structure.[26] When we consider, thinking mainly of librarianship, how greatly the ability to deliver services has been enhanced by the development of automation, itself a late development of the industrial division of labor and closely associated with the rise of the more complex forms of social organization, this is not at all surprising. The reason we are taken aback at first is probably that most of us in some way still harbor an older, largely mythical image of a professional as a person who works independently of large organizations. Librarians, of course, are less likely than others to share this myth, for the larger and more comprehensive collections have always shown a relatively high degree of bureaucratization. Nonetheless, librarians who work in these complex organizations have more resources to work with, more support personnel, bigger budgets, and a greater freedom to expand the scope of their services. No doubt they also enjoy a higher level of general social recognition than librarians who work in smaller and less visible settings.

This contrast between the older and the more recent professional style is fundamental. In the nineteenth century the religious, medical, legal, and scientific professions provided the stock examples of the independent professional: Trollope's curates and vicars, living and working in their isolated country parishes and regarding their bishops with often ill-concealed suspicion; or literary medical heroes like Sinclair Lewis's Doc Kennicott and Martin Arrowsmith. The image of Abraham Lincoln, teaching himself to write by firelight on the back of a spade and "reading for the law," is far from the contemporary equivalent of entering the field; equally quaint by our standards are the images of such inventors as Robert Fulton and Thomas Edison working in relative isolation. What all of these have in common is the older idea of the professional working independently of complex organizations. The contemporary professional, however, is from the beginning a member of a highly organized group, or even a series of such groups: the professional school (involving a complex set of relationships with students, teachers, and administrators); the occupation itself, with many thousands of colleagues, numerous subgroups and interest groups, including many different kinds of professional associations; and the organization within which the work is done: library, law firm, hospital, government agency, corporation, school, and so on.

PROFESSIONS AND CLASS CONFLICT

The social class dimension of professional work is relatively clear, for it seems obvious that the typical concerns of professional or professionalizing workers are predominantly middle class.[27] Issues like autonomy or the use of formal education in work are certainly more commonly diffused throughout the occupational structure than they were at one time, but they are less common in working-class circles. If it is true that some of the concerns of middle-class workers have spread elsewhere, it is also true that the middle-class occupations show evidence of class conflict, often thought to be a purely "blue collar" preoccupation. Most of us immediately recognize the organizational activities of unions as part of class conflict in industrial society, but we are slower to see this as an essential factor in the development of a profession. The altruistic, at times self-congratulatory, language of official pronouncements, ethics codes, association reports, and in-house histories must be seen at least partly as a fight for a certain set of occupational interests. Thus, as Goode points out, the attempt to procure professional status is a keenly competitive process, elitist in form, which has for its major goal the appropriation of social rewards through restriction of access to privileged kinds of work. Naturally only a few occupational groups will achieve the greatest level of success in doing this—scarcity itself is one of the conditions of value.[28]

Despite the mystification of the class conflict dimension of the professionalization process, it is clear upon examination that it is exclusivist as well as elitist in nature. Viewed positively, the defense of occupational interests is an attempt to protect one's field of work. But viewed negatively, it is also an attempt to exclude allegedly "unqualified" others from the rewards of practice. Since professional workers are usually drawn from middle-class and upper-middle-class populations, their attempt at exclusion has a strong flavor of class-based domination. Middle-class occupations with liberal ideologies attached to them may be especially slow to recognize the class conflict factor, and librarians are strongly centered on traditional liberalism. Nevertheless, the occupation of librarianship is overwhelmingly white and overwhelmingly middle-class and upper-middle-class in composition.[29]

CONCLUSION

This chapter sketches in a very general way the rise of the professions as a part of the overall development of contemporary society; and it situates the appearance of the information occupations and the "bibliographic sector" in this larger context. Though remaining in certain ways rooted in the ancient traditions of work in preindustrial societies, the professions as we think of them today, particularly in the United States and Great Britain, are rather different from their earlier forms.[30] They were in large part forged in the crucible of industrialism; and like adults whose mature features occasionally recall the world of childhood that produced them, they bear the marks of the formative period. Once closely linked with the magical, the sacred, and the mysterious, professional work emerged from the early industrial period with a transformed identity: highly specialized, sophisticated, collegially organized, and linked in numerous and complex ways to equally transformed institutions of higher learning. Further, it was inescapably linked with the advance of the sciences, theoretical and applied, physical and social. And like many other kinds of work, it gained a distinctly cosmopolitan flavor, as it lost many of the older ties to local cultures.

In the next three chapters we look at three different, if sometimes related, views of professions. Chapter 2 examines the trait theory; Chapter 3 turns to the functionalist and occupational control approaches; and in Chapter 4 the findings of the occupational control model are applied to librarianship.

The trait theory comes first since it was an early attempt, but also because it has a special relationship to the material discussed in this chapter. In the formative period of the modern professions, it was natural for professionals to feel threatened by the rise of industrialism, and equally natural for them to respond to that threat by proposing lists of "traits" that could be used as instruments for proving their own claims to professional status as well as excluding other groups from moving in on their turf. If the first wave of sociologists who turned to the professions as a field of study seem, from today's viewpoint, to have overemphasized these traits and to have put too much stress on the winning of social status, this is in part because the early environment of professionalism was highly preoccupied with these issues. And so we turn now to a closer look at the first systematic attempt to understand the modern professional occupations.

NOTES

1. See, for example, Burton Bledstein, *The Culture of Professionalism* (New York: Norton, 1976), pp. 36–39, and (for a detailed breakdown of the earlier attempts at occupational classification) Theodore Caplow, *The Sociology of Work* (Minneapolis: University of Minnesota Press, 1954). Recent analyses of census data show this to be a very long term trend. See C. B. Di Cesare, "Changes in the Occupational Structure of U.S. Jobs," *Monthly Labor Review* 98, 3 (March 1975): 24–34.

2. For a more detailed discussion of the historical background of the relation between the modern occupational structure and the division of labor in industrial societies, see Elliot A. Krause, *The Sociology of Occupations* (Boston: Little, Brown, 1971), pp. 13ff., 29, 60ff. The relationship between the "traditional learned professions" and the medieval university is part of the background of the struggle for prestige in more modern times, where newer professional groups seek university affiliation. See Eliot Freidson, "The Theory of the Professions: State of the Art," *The Sociology of the Professions: Doctors, Lawyers, and Others*, eds. Robert Dingwall and Philip Lewis (London: Macmillan, 1983), p. 24.

3. Don Martindale, *The Nature and Types of Sociological Theory* (Boston: Houghton Mifflin), pp. 440ff. See also Eliot Freidson, "Are Professions Necessary?" *The Authority of Experts: Studies in History and Theory*, ed. Thomas L. Haskell (Bloomington: Indiana University Press, 1984), pp. 4–12. For a historical account of the rise of the social sciences in the United States in relation to industrialization, see Mary O. Furner, *Advocacy and Objectivity: A Crisis in the Professionalization of American Social Science, 1865–1905* (Lexington: University Press of Kentucky, 1975), pp. 1, 10–15, 21–22. Christopher Lasch in a similar way covers the rise of family sociology in *Haven in a Heartless World* (New York: Basic Books, 1977).

4. See Werner Jaeger, *Paideia: The Ideals of Greek Culture*, vol. 3, trans. Gilbert Highet (New York: Oxford University Press, 1945), pp. 3–44, where it is argued that Greek medicine formed part of the ancient background of the Ionian scientific movement.

5. For these and other details of "natural history," see Harold Wilensky, "The Professionalization of Everyone?" *American Journal of Sociology* 70 (September 1964): 143. It is worth noting, however, that even though the American Library Association was founded in the historic year of 1876, "the first convention of library enthusiasts had been held in 1853 in New York," and this pushes the earliest phase of professionalization somewhat further back than is commonly thought. In this, librarianship was following a rather common pattern in the period between 1850 and 1880, for there were clear signs of similar development in many other occupations in the United States: dentists, dairymen, photographers, lawyers, chemists, mathematicians, and many others. See Dee Garrison, *Apostles of Culture: The Public Librarian and American Society, 1876–1920* (New York: Free Press, 1979), pp. 3–7.

6. Georges Gurvitsch, *The Social Frameworks of Knowledge*, trans. Margaret A. Thompson and Kenneth A. Thompson (Oxford: Blackwell, 1971). The theoretical connection between the rise of modern occupations and their attendant knowledge bases was first explored by Karl Mannheim, in *Ideology and Utopia: Introduction to the Sociology of Knowledge*, trans. Louis Wirth and Edward Shils (New York: Harcourt, Brace, 1936).

7. "Bibliographical R & D," *The Study of Information: Interdisciplinary Messages*, eds. Fritz Machlup and Una Mansfield (New York: Wiley, 1983), pp. 390ff.

8. The importance of printing in helping to bring about this and other changes is the subject of an exhaustive study by Elizabeth Eisenstein, *The Printing Press as an Agent of Change*, 2 vols. (Cambridge: Cambridge University Press, 1979).

9. See Leigh Estabrook, ed., *Libraries and Post-Industrial Society* (Phoenix, AZ: Oryx Press, 1977).

10. The interplay of the types of knowledge is a subject for the history and philosophy of science. For example, the stock of commonsense knowledge, amorphous and yet sharply relevant to a wide variety of ordinary concerns, is relative to the historical period and the general state of scientific knowledge at the time; and since both of these change constantly, the sphere of practical knowledge is not at all easy to control. On the historical relativity of commonsense knowledge, see W. V. O. Quine, *Word and Object* (Cambridge, MA: MIT Press, 1960), and by the same author, *Ontological Relativity, and Other Essays* (New York: Columbia University Press, 1969).

11. Abraham Kaplan, "The Age of the Symbol—A Philosophy of Library Education," *The Intellectual Foundations of Library Education*, ed. Don R. Swanson (Chicago: University of Chicago Press, 1965), p. 13. For an application of the idea of the obsolescence of bibliophilia in the context of collection management, see Marcia Pankake, "From Book Selection to Collection Management: Continuity and Advance in an Unending Work," *Advances In Librarianship* 13 (1984): 185–210.

12. Patrick Wilson, "Bibliographical R & D," p. 396.

13. In recent years, three important attempts at metascientific understanding are structuralism, semiotics, and systems theory, each developed as a common framework for understanding human activity generally, and for understanding knowledge in particular. Structuralism, for example, has been applied to fields as widely varied as biology, literature, religion, sociology, anthropology, and linguistics; some anthropologists clearly view it as a master science. See, for example, Claude Levi-Strauss, *Structural Anthropology*, trans. Claire Jacobson and Brooke Schoepf (New York: Basic Books, 1963). A statement of the general viewpoint and a general theory of semiotics can be found in Umberto Eco, *A Theory of Semiotics* (Bloomington: Indiana University Press, 1976); for a general overview of systems theory, see among many others, Ervin Laszlo, *The Systems View of the World* (New York: Braziller, 1972). The general background of my use of the term *metascience* is from Gerhard Radnitzky, *Contemporary Schools of Metascience* (Chicago: Henry Regnery, 1973).

14. For example, Lois Mai Chan, "Dewey 18: Another Step in the Evolutionary Process," *Library Resources and Technical Services* 16 (Summer 1972): 383–99.

15. Jose Ortega y Gasset, "The Mission of the Librarian," *Antioch Review* 21 (Summer 1961): 133–54.

16. Weber's model of bureaucratic organization includes a hierarchy of offices, fixed jurisdiction, specialized training of officials, the existence of written or printed files, and a formal chain of command. Max Weber, *From Max Weber: Essays in Sociology*, trans. and eds. H. H. Gerth and C. Wright Mills (New York: Oxford University Press, 1958). Many of the criticisms that have been made of Weber's theory of bureaucracy are summarized in Peter Blau and Marshall Meyer, *Bureaucracy and Modern Society*, 3rd ed. (New York: Free Press, 1987).

17. *The Collected Poems of W. B. Yeats* (New York: Macmillan, 1956), p. 7.

18. Durkheim's argument is in *The Division of Labor in Society*, trans. George Simpson (New York: Macmillan, 1960). For a brief summary see George Simpson, ed., *Emile Durkheim: Selections from His Work* (New York: Thomas Crowell, 1963), pp. 45–69.

Weber's arguments are diffused through a large body of work and not easy to summarize, but a good introductory statement can be found in *From Max Weber*, pp. 45–65. Durkheim was preceded in the argument involving the division of labor by Spencer, who recognized its importance for social integration. See C. Turner and M. N. Hodge, "Occupations and Professions," *Professions and Professionalisation*, ed. John Archer Jackson (Cambridge: Cambridge University Press, 1970), pp. 17–50. For a historical account that translates many of these theoretical ideas into terms that apply directly to the rise of industrial society in the United States in the latter part of the nineteenth century, see Robert Wiebe, *The Search for Order, 1877–1920* (New York: Hill and Wang, 1967).

19. The *locus classicus* is John Stuart Mill's *On Liberty*, first published in 1859 and discussed at length in Isaiah Berlin, *Four Essays on Liberty* (New York: Oxford University Press, 1969).

20. W. Richard Scott, "Professionals in Bureaucracies—Areas of Conflict," *Professionalization*, eds. Howard Vollmer and Donald Mills (Englewood Cliffs, NJ: Prentice-Hall, 1966), pp. 265–75; also Talcott Parsons, "Professions," *The International Encyclopedia of the Social Sciences* (New York: Macmillan, 1968).

21. *Division of Labor in Society*, pp. 131ff. The argument is much expanded in Durkheim's *Professional Ethics and Civic Morals*, trans. Cornelia Brookfield (Glencoe, IL: Free Press, 1958).

22. These characteristics, or "traits," are found in numerous sources, including Ernest Greenwood, "Attributes of a Profession," *Social Work* 2, 3 (July 1957): 45ff.; Wilensky, "Professionalization of Everyone?" pp. 137–58; William J. Goode, "The Theoretical Limits of Professionalization," *The Semi-Professions and Their Organization*, ed. Amitai Etzioni (New York: Free Press, 1969), pp. 266–313; and Eliot Freidson, ed., *The Professions and Their Prospects* (Beverly Hills: Sage Publications, 1975).

23. Talcott Parsons, *Essays in Sociological Theory, Pure and Applied* (Glencoe, IL: Free Press, 1949), pp. 34–39. The original line between professional service and the profit orientation is still valid, but is now more difficult to draw, given the great expansion in the field of services generally. The institutionalization of the service occupations in reference to librarianship is discussed by Jody Newmyer, "The Image Problem of the Librarian: Femininity and Social Control," *Journal of Library History* 11 (January 1976): 44–67.

24. See Gloria V. Engel, "Professional Autonomy and Bureaucratic Organization," *Administrative Science Quarterly* 15 (March 1970): 12–21; and John B. Cullen, *The Structure of Professionalism: A Quantitative Examination* (New York: Petrocelli, 1978), p. 8.

25. The exception is "technical competence," which does make sense intuitively. See Richard Hall, "Professionalization and Bureaucratization," *American Sociological Review* 33 (February 1968): 103.

26. Beverly Lynch, "Libraries as Bureaucracies," *Library Trends* 27 (Winter 1979): 260.

27. Magali S. Larson, *The Rise of Professionalism: A Sociological Analysis* (Berkeley: University of California Press, 1977), pp. 186, 239; and Vernon K. Dibble, "Occupations and Ideologies," *The Sociology of Knowledge: A Reader*, eds. James E. Curtis and John W. Petras (New York: Praeger, 1970), pp. 436–42.

28. William J. Goode, "The Librarian: From Occupation to Profession?" *Library Quarterly* 31 (October 1961): 306–20.

29. Robert D. Stueart, in "Education for Librarianship: The Way It Is." *ALA Yearbook*

of Library and Information Services '84 (Chicago: American Library Association, 1983), p. 4, makes it clear that librarianship's student population is still more than 97 percent white. The social class composition of the field is not easy to document, though obvious enough to casual observation, which may indicate that it is one of the buried problems in research on the profession. Even a relatively recent survey fails to mention social class at all in discussing background characteristics of professional workers. See L. S. Estabrook and K. M. Heim, "Profile of ALA Members," *American Libraries* 11 (December 1980): 654–59. It may be that researchers are assuming that since the field is predominantly female, class background should be traced through significant males—husbands or fathers, for example. But since the issue seems not to be discussed, it remains a mystery, at least as far as the present is concerned. The historical record, on the other hand, is clearer, and the predominantly middle- and upper-middle-class backgrounds of librarians in the earliest period of American librarianship is evident in Dee Garrison's *Apostles of Culture: The Public Librarian and American Society, 1876–1920* (New York: Free Press, 1979), pp. xii–xiii, 17–20.

30. Professions in Europe, particularly in France, Germany, and Italy, have followed such a different pattern that this qualification is essential. One major difference is in the connection between professional education and national university programs. For details, see Eliot Freidson, "Theory of the Professions: State of the Art," pp. 22ff.

2

Early Efforts: The Emergence of the Trait Theory

Chapter 1 treats the professions in a very general historical and sociological way, but it makes no specific reference to a theory or a definition of professionalism. In this and the following chapter, we move from these background issues to the three major theories of the sociology of professional work: the trait theory, the functionalist theory, and the occupational control approach.

The trait theory is the view, simply put, that a profession is an occupation with certain characteristics. Naturally there is disagreement on which traits are most central, whether or not they can be ranked, how or in what precise temporal order the traits are acquired or displayed by an occupation—all of these have at one time or other been the subject of controversy. But before entering into any of these areas, we need to underline the simple fact that all of these views have in common the idea that it is possible to list an occupation's characteristics and thus judge its claim to professional status. Versions of the trait theory also seem to share a key assumption, the idea that there is a state of being—a rather exalted one—called "full professionalization," and that the most traditional and longest established professional groups have attained this state.

Actually there are two versions of the trait theory, one we may call the "pure trait theory" and the other the "natural history" theory.[1] They share the view that discovering the essential qualities of professionalism is the crux of the study of the professions. The pure trait theory starts with a list of characteristics, usually specifies one or more traits as essential, may or may not attempt to compare various occupations against the checklist, and sometimes concludes with a judgment for or against a given occupation's "claim" to be considered a profession. The natural history theory, however, suggests in addition that the traits are generally acquired in a certain sequence, which is itself an important part of the notion of professionalization. In fact, the natural history theory holds that the order of acquisition of the traits *is* the professionalizing process.[2]

Although it is relatively easy to distinguish between the two versions of the theory, in fact there is a strong tendency for most trait approaches to involve, sooner or later, reference to an allegedly "natural" sequence of steps in the professionalizing process. When we look at one of the clearer examples of the natural history theory, we find, furthermore, that there is really only one possible sequence involved, as if the theory were based on a kind of fatal inevitability, similar to the sense of inevitability found in the older ideas of social progress: "Many occupations engage in heroic struggles for professional identification; few make the grade."[3] What then, according to the natural history version of the trait theory, are these necessary steps, and how are they related in a sequence?

There is, first, the emergence of the occupation as a full-time pursuit—a vocation as opposed to an avocation, or the emergence of the "professional" as opposed to the "amateur." Originally there was no implicit claim of moral superiority as there is today where "amateurism" is usually regarded with disdain or outright contempt. The importance of this aspect of professionalism generally lies in the fact that the professional, unlike the amateur, has a particularly serious form of commitment to the job and cannot ignore its claims, unless he or she is willing to seek an entirely different line of work. Again in contrast to amateurs, professionals pay close attention to patrons, clients, or users of their services, and thus define their interests in relation to the needs of service. An amateur, on the other hand, pursues an interest out of love for the subject and may have no concern for the needs of any particular group of people. In fact, in certain now largely obsolete forms of professionalism, the user of the services exercised an absolute control over the professional's work.[4]

The other traits follow in a predictable order. The emergence of full-time pursuit and its commitments precedes the appearance of the first training school; somewhat later the school seeks university affiliation. The university-based school generally appears before the founding of the professional association, because the formal association is a response to the needs of trained professionals to discuss common interests, sponsor activities that encourage practitioners to advance in their knowledge, protect the field from outsiders, and all of the other functions such agencies routinely fulfill. In some cases, of course, this order does not hold true. For example, in librarianship, the reverse is the case; the association came first, encouraged the formation of the training schools, and pushed for university affiliation.[5]

The next step in the process is a phase of political agitation whose primary goal is to win legal support for the protection of the occupation from outside competition, or "encroachment." Without legal support for its positions, the association lacks the strongest kind of social support for its claims of expertise. Official examinations, licensing, and certification—perhaps even special directives like residence rules—are part of this phase of development. In the supposedly typical pattern, licensing and certification come, if at all, toward the end of the political activism period. Eventually the drive toward political power and legal legitimacy, its goals achieved, turns to the problem of self-regulation in the form of the ethics code.[6] If we follow the general logic of this view, the code of ethics is a "good faith" gesture confirming the occupation's worthiness and responsibility and assuring the public that the right to control itself is merited.

The natural history theory does not, of course, have a spot for every trait that has at one time or another been used in understanding the professions; there are simply too many to try and arrange in one sequence. In addition to the full-time occupation, the training school, the affiliation with the university, the association, legal protection, and the ethics code, other versions of the trait theory put heavy emphasis on additional traits. First, and perhaps most important, is the knowledge base: the theoretical and practical body of techniques, principles, general ideas, and values on which practice is based. Some minimal mastery of this body of knowledge is required for entry into practice. Although not always made explicit, there is an assumption that the body of knowledge requires a specialized group of teachers and scholars to maintain it. Second, and closely related to the knowledge base, is the characteristic of autonomy, or the ability to exercise control over the work process. Third and fourth—already noted in the natural history theory—are the association and the ethics code. Two additional traits frequently mentioned are the service orientation and the recognition of the community of those who will use the service. Finally, a trait of great importance, frequently omitted from direct consideration but always implicit in any discussion of the professions, is the presence of a "professional culture."[7]

It is not possible to look in detail at every trait, or to reconstruct historically all the different possibilities of sequence. Instead we focus on a smaller set of core traits. Thus, in the following sections we consider the knowledge base, the relation between professional knowledge and autonomy, the professional association, the ethics code, the concept of service to clients, and the social recognition of the wider community. The concept of a professional culture is discussed in Chapter 8 in connection with suggestions for research.

THE KNOWLEDGE BASE: THEORY AND PRACTICE

Probably because "profession" is traditionally so frequently contrasted with various kinds of manual and semiskilled labor, the knowledge base has received a lot of attention in the trait theory. Indeed, the development of a body of theoretical knowledge—closely allied to the university professional or graduate school—would have to be recognized by anyone, trait theorist or not, as central to what we call professional work. Without it, an occupation would be based on a set of technical routines or on no intellectual skills at all. The problem of defining and evaluating the knowledge base of an occupation is not at all easy, for there is an essential ambiguity in professional knowledge. A delicate balance of breadth and depth must be struck: too broad, and its generality approaches commonsense knowledge; too narrow, and it does not really require significant theoretical ability to master it.[8] There is, in other words, an essential "indeterminacy" of the knowledge base, for it must fall somewhere between the purely general and the purely technical or specific. In addition, the knowledge base achieves an esoteric quality simply because of the high degree of specialization in the occupational structure: it remains hidden from others. Indeterminacy and the inevitable social distance created by a highly differentiated social structure combine to make professional knowledge frequently appear opaque to outsiders.[9]

Narrowness in the knowledge base is, in the long run, probably more of a block to professionalization than breadth, since it discourages the formation of imaginative, problem-solving habits of mind, which in turn makes it easier for persons outside the occupation to control its activities. In the past librarianship has sometimes been regarded as based on very general types of knowledge, whereas information science, if anything, would be put toward the overly specific end of the continuum. More recently these two areas seem to be moving closer together, perhaps so that the generality of the one can complement the specificity of the other, and thus reach an acceptably indeterminate compromise. In any case, there is evidence of considerable theoretical development in the core areas of library and information science, as shown by some recent work in the theory of bibliography.[10] This, however, is only one area of possible examples. Others can be found in the development of classification and indexing, now a vast and complex theoretical field, and in the application of the methods of the historical and behavioral sciences to the study of user behavior, and of quantitative methods to the study of bodies of literature.

The connection between theory and practice in different kinds of human activity varies considerably. In professional knowledge, it should be much closer than it is in pure research disciplines. In the professions, practice comes first, both in fact and in principle; and in the professions, practice serves, in a much more immediate sense, as a test of theory. On the other hand, this does not mean that whatever happens in practice is automatically superior to whatever is announced in theory. It means only that developments in knowledge have improvements in service as their main reason for being.

The Application of Pure Knowledge

The application of pure knowledge is easier to grasp through a contrast with the relationship between theory and practice in the traditional academic disciplines. For example, in philosophy, the social sciences, and the natural sciences widely varying degrees of closeness can be found in the relationship between the knowledge and its influence on ordinary affairs. Sometimes the connection is extremely strong, even in fields thought to be too recondite to matter to ordinary people. One example is philosophy.

Philosophical knowledge is generally cultivated by itself and applied within its own limits by a self-sufficient group of scholars. No doubt there will always be a core of philosophical thought that refers only to its own concerns. But philosophy has often been applied to very concrete problems; ethics is an illustration. The pure ethics of contemporary philosophy have recently been applied to medicine, business, and law.

The same could be done for the library profession by using ethical research to clarify problems of intellectual freedom. For example, consider the old debate between the traditional liberal and the idealistic views of freedom—basically the difference between the negative and the positive views of freedom. For the liberal, the only freedom is "freedom from" outside interference. For the idealist, however, the concept of freedom needs to be filled in with something positive; it must be viewed as a "freedom to" act in certain ways, and it must lead to the realization of some value. This contrast can illuminate the ongoing debate on pornography and the exploitation of women and children, an issue that ought to be very close to the concerns of many librarians. The current radical and conservative coalition that is stridently questioning the ability of liberalism to deal with this issue is partly based on an idealist critique of negative freedom. Negative freedom, this argument holds, allows the exploitation of women and children in pornography, and thus indirectly legitimates it. If negative freedom underlies one's philosophy of intellectual freedom, this creates some very practical problems.

In the social sciences the connection between seemingly pure knowledge and practice gets considerably closer because there is a closer connection between social science and social policy than there is between philosophy and public affairs. But this connection is not only intellectual, for its probably reflects the common origins, as noted in Chapter 1, of the social sciences and the concern with social policy in the industrial period. There are many examples in this area. For instance, the sociology of the family and the sociology of sex roles are both used, sometimes quite directly, in proposing or arguing against changes in legislative or administrative policy. This is also true of research on ethnic relations, poverty, and many other areas. For example, the Moynihan Report, on the sociology of the black family, generated much social policy debate and was used to create federal programs designed to strengthen minority family structure. Another example is the influence of social scientists on the 1954 Supreme Court decision in Brown vs. The Board of Education.[11] Each of these examples shows quite clearly that specialized scholarly debates can very quickly become the center of intense public concern.

In the natural sciences and technical fields the connection becomes even closer, in part because a great deal of the research in these areas is funded for specific practical purposes. Since there is so much money available to fund scientific research, particularly in the health sciences, there are many examples, such as the development of genetic engineering as an applied form of biochemistry. Here again, the closeness of the connection has, at least in part, to do with the historical importance of the role of the natural sciences in the rise of industrialism.

The Application of Knowledge in the Professions

When we look at the professions, however, we come to an essentially different type of relationship between theory and practice. Here it is not so much a question of a historical relationship offering opportunities for commercial or political exploitation. It is not a question of an intellectually perceptive business or government elite recognizing a useful development, although this does happen in professional knowledge. It is rather that, in the professions, knowledge is produced almost entirely for practical purposes. Today, enterprising scholars from the pure research disciplines are indeed borrowing ideas from the professions, but generally speaking professional knowledge makers develop these ideas because some problem in the delivery of services requires attention, not because the ideas are in themselves "interesting."

In librarianship the need to develop a relevant body of knowledge has the important complication that the knowledge must by itself provide clues to the organization of human knowledge generally, at least in its recorded forms. To do this, of course, a good deal of the type of knowledge that is more common in other professional fields must also be produced, emphasizing direct services to clients. In librarianship there is simultaneously a need to organize records of knowledge generally—already a huge task by itself—and to study the needs of particular user groups. It is difficult to perform both of these functions, and so the broader function is usually shortcut in favor of the more immediate needs of users, and its own knowledge base may thus be neglected. Instead, it becomes practical to organize the knowledge bases of other disciplines and make those records available. (This is reflected in the ironic fact that frequently the literature of library science is far less accessible, from the point of view of bibliographic organization, than the literature of many other fields.)

Of course, the effect of this is that librarianship's own knowledge base is pushed closer and closer to the narrow or technical end, no doubt a characteristic of most of the occupations of the "bibliographic sector." As Patrick Wilson points out, both librarianship and information science tend to focus on "work aimed at improving the means of storage, manipulation, transmission, and display of bibliographical information, based on the application of computer technology."[12] Thus, "immediate access" tends to win out over longer term development of the field as a form of metascience, and this more theoretical development proceeds at a much slower rate. This fact notwithstanding, there is no convincing evidence for the prima facie rejection of librarianship's claim to have a body of "theoretical knowledge" upon which to base its practice, for there is, in fact, a significant body of research literature that has accumulated over the past century.[13]

PROFESSIONAL KNOWLEDGE AND PROFESSIONAL AUTONOMY

In the professions, knowledge has a direct connection to power, for it enables professionals to control many of the basic aspects of their work. When cultivated, the knowledge base of a profession grows, and when it grows, it brings with it a certain control over routines. This intellectual and occupational power does not automatically or immediately confer social, economic, or political power, and it does not automatically bring greater material rewards. But it does bring control of the work within the grasp of those who use the knowledge to serve its publics.

The development of the knowledge base of the occupation is thus closely linked with its ability to maintain autonomy in practice, since the breadth and depth of the knowledge prevent outsiders from easily mastering its application. Much of the reason for the continuing development of professional knowledge is to prevent encroachment—to keep outsiders from poaching on one's preserve— but the importance of the knowledge base has philosophical and moral dimensions as well. This has to do with the use of the imagination in work: the ability to examine problems in the abstract. It is a form of intellectual craftsmanship. The mastery of a theoretical body of knowledge is thus not restricted to the application of principles, for it includes insight into the formation of the principles themselves and the assumptions underlying them. The moral dimension of the exercise of the imagination lies with the sense of professional responsibility that comes from the ability to solve problems creatively in the interests of those who lack the skills to do so themselves.

To summarize, there are three aspects of autonomy emphasized here: practical, philosophical, and moral. The practical—perhaps one could almost say "political"—aspect is rooted in the need to use the knowledge base to restrict practice and the use of relevant skills to certain practitioners accepted as legitimate. And although this has a distinctly selfish ring to it, it has its altruistic side also, for the restriction of practice protects clients from unscrupulous or improperly trained practitioners. The philosophical part of autonomy is the free use of the imagination to solve problems: a professional is a person who can solve many different kinds of client-related problems because he or she can entertain solutions intellectually, without needing to subject each one to trial and error. Part of this ability lies with the scope of experience, but it is really the use of the imagination that is central, for without it the professional is tied to what has in fact happened and cannot deal with the much wider world of possibility.

The use of the imagination suggests a radical kind of freedom, but the real freedom of the professional is situated in a corporate context, limited and otherwise checked by relations with colleagues, as well as by generally accepted moral principles. Thus, while the imagination inclines to a relatively individualistic notion of freedom, the situated actions that occur in work are really based on an idea of autonomy that has an essential reference to the occupation as a whole. When we speak of "professional freedom," then, we are not speaking of the freedom of this or that professional person, but rather of the corporate freedom of the group. One consequence of this is that professionals, even when they exhibit a high degree of independence, are not by any means absolutely free to use knowledge as they wish; they must accept limitations on that freedom from shared standards. Put another way, if "freedom" suggests individual license, "autonomy" suggests a kind of individual freedom that is situated in an organized occupational group. Thus the idea of autonomy presupposed in professional work, although rooted in the liberalism and radical individualism of seventeenth- and eighteenth-century political philosophy, really represents a modern version of an old compromise between freedom and social responsibility.[14]

ASSOCIATIONS

The professional association is important for governance, standard-setting, and for its role in the promotion of scholarship leading to the development of the knowledge base. It is also critical in the formation of the professional culture, for it is one of the sources of shared orientations toward work. As a whole, the American Library Association (ALA) is less oriented toward research than are some other professional associations; in many ways it is more like a trade association than a learned society or a professional group,[15] although in part this is a reflection of its size and extremely diverse membership. Specialized groups within the ALA, such as the Library History Round Table, the Library Research Round Table, and the Association of College and Research Libraries, fulfill a range of scholarly and professional functions.

Associations of professional workers originally found in certain medieval occupations had a structure that closely resembled similar organizations for skilled craftsmen.[16] Indeed, the contemporary professional association may well be rooted in medieval guild organization. Some clergymen, however, as members of a church, were not free to "associate" with fellow workers in the sense of direct participation in activities outside the parent institution.[17] Early on, associations of professionals were openly and stridently moralistic in their attempts to "curb the audacity of unskilled knaves"—partly a reference to self-protection but no doubt also reflecting concern for the safety of clients.[18] In the seventeenth and eighteenth centuries a powerful antiprofessional sentiment developed, labeling the associations as corrupt secret societies perpetrating nonsense and hiding abuse and incompetence. Familiar examples are Molière's caricatures of physicians in his plays: "explaining" to a patient that opium makes us sleep because it has "dormative powers." Partly in answer to such criticism, a more responsive, reform-oriented association began to appear.

The other significant factor in the rise of the modern professional associations was the increasing demand for autonomy on the part of practitioners. Originally subject to the virtually absolute authority of powerful patrons, professionals developed an increasing freedom to define how services should be delivered and began to ask large questions about the values underlying service.[19] It is not accidental that the gradual development of the association as a protector of worker autonomy coincides with the period in which the growth of the sciences stimulated industrial growth, for the ideal of professional autonomy rests on an idea of intellectual freedom that has much in common with the idea of free scientific inquiry. From this point on, professional workers increasingly looked to their associations as protectors of their freedom.

Most of the functions we think of as significant were present in these early forms, including guaranteeing competence, devising means to test it, and presenting positive evidence to the public. Closely related to monitoring competence was, and is, the concern with raising the level of that competence and assuring the public that standards are being met. Associations of all kinds shared the problem of raising the social prestige level of the occupation, for in the medieval and early modern periods, until the time of the industrial revolution, professional people were very low in social standing. In comparison with the titled and the noble, professionals were little better than "tradesmen." Thus the battle for higher status and greater social recognition is a very old one.[20]

Although there is clearly a family resemblance between contemporary professional associations and those of an earlier time, there is an important difference. It has much to do with the increasing demand for autonomy; contemporary associations are not only freer from patron influence but also much less hierarchically organized than were the medieval guilds. They do have their levels of authority and their inequalities of status—they are clearly dominated by certain identifiable interests—but these are much less pronounced than they once were, and indeed less pronounced than most contemporary work settings. And this, of course, is one of their most appealing features, for it gives practitioners an opportunity to participate directly in the life of the group, something that may not be possible in a highly bureaucratized work organization.

ETHICS CODES: VALUES, RIGHTS, AND SANCTIONS

The development of ethics codes articulating values and principles affecting the conduct of workers, especially in the area of professional/client relations, frequently lags behind other developments. The American Library Association did not develop an official code until 1938, some sixty years after its formation. And this practice is not at all unusual, for there are, according to a study in the late 1970s, a large number of professional associations that have no ethics codes at all. In part this reflects the fact that it is sometimes difficult to draw the line between a professional association and a learned society, and certainly the absence of ethics codes is more pronounced in the latter group. Still, this is a surprising finding, since many of these societies are directly concerned with human subjects research.[21]

It is often observed that the authority of the association is reflected in the code, and in the official reaction to infractions. This is probably true, but there is a great deal of variation in the severity of the reaction against practitioners who violate the code. In part this depends on the importance that professionals attach to maintaining a monopoly over their services, which in turn reflects the degree to which the occupation may be threatened by competition.[22] But it is also determined by historical factors and by the organizational peculiarities of different occupations, and no doubt also by general social and cultural values. For example, in the clergy violations have overtones of blasphemy, and although the situations are somewhat different in law and medicine, there is also some of the same feeling of "sacredness" that affects how violators will be treated.

Librarians, on the other hand, generally deal with the "profane," but there is nonetheless enough reverence for knowledge to make violations of intellectual freedom very serious matters.

The business of authority and sanctions and dealing with violators of the code is certainly important, but perhaps somewhat overstated in view of the fact that relatively few workers engage in serious violations or need formal discipline. What is more significant is the positive function of translating moral values into a set of principles governing the conduct of the average worker in complex or ambiguous situations. Problems dealt with by codes generally fall into three areas: relationships between professionals and clients, between colleagues, and between colleagues and employers. Usually it is the professional/client area that receives the most attention. An example in librarianship is the question of confidentiality of circulation records, which is directly parallel to the confidentiality of client records in medical and legal work. Relations between colleagues also involve confidentiality, although of a different kind. And, of course, relations between professional workers and their employers or employing organizations at times produce some of the most difficult problems of right and ownership (for example, with inventions, patents, licenses, copyright interests).

Ethics codes are made up of specific principles, values, sanctions brought to bear on the enforcement of conduct, and the rights of professionals and clients that the code is designed to protect. When we think of professional ethics codes informally, we are usually thinking of specific principles such as "Everyone has a right to a defense in a court of law," or "No one shall be denied essential medical treatment." Principles are propositions that place basic values in a logical relationship and say something in a general way that regulates professional behavior. *Value* is used here to mean a quality of life or experience held to be intrinsically good. The term *sanction* refers to a positive or negative inducement to express, through one's professional behavior, a basic agreement with the principles and values expressed in the code. *Right* means "guarantee of access to the enjoyment of some value." And so there will be, roughly speaking, a right corresponding to each area of value: a right to know or have the chance to inquire, a right to justice, a right to health and dignity, and so on.

In librarianship, and to a still largely undetermined degree in the other occupations of the bibliographic sector, typical values are knowledge, free inquiry, intellectual and creative expression, truth, and toleration. (Toleration may be an example of an orientation that is both intrinsically and extrinsically valued.) Typical examples of rights are freedom of expression, freedom of access to information, freedom to read, and so on. Sanctions are generally informal, consisting of strongly held shared views among librarians that preexist entry into the profession and are reinforced by library school and work experiences.

In law, justice is the basic value, and the corresponding rights reflect this emphasis. Typical examples of client rights are the right to counsel and the right to be informed of one's rights. In the legal profession, sanctions are both informal—as in librarianship, interaction with peers and the professional school experience—but, unlike librarianship, are also formally expressed in explicit control mechanisms: lawyers who don't obey the code can be disbarred or punished as criminals. In medicine, the basic values are health and life, and recently there has been great controversy on the link between the two. For the most part, physicians no longer regard mere existence as of unquestionable value. Another recent change is that the value of "dignity" has taken on an importance roughly equal to the older values of health and life. Client rights include the right to treatment as well as the right to refuse treatment (at least for oneself). As with law, sanctions are a combination of the formal and the informal: interaction with peers, educational experiences, early exposure to work routines, and formal legal controls found, for example, in governmental regulation of medical practice.

The distinction drawn here between informal and formal sanctions in ethics codes is actually a reflection of a more fundamental distinction between types of social control in professional work. Although the point cannot be covered in detail here, it should be noted that informal and formal means of ensuring conformity to the code each contribute, although in different ways, to maintaining an occupational style that flavors the interaction between professional and client. In some cases, librarianship for example, informal sanctions and a correspondingly informal occupational organization predominate; in others, control occurs by a mixing of types. The fact that the types coexist in certain groups is enough to show that they are not mutually exclusive. What is not always appreciated is the effectiveness and strength of informal sanctions, even when operating by themselves. Even without legal support, informal control assures a high degree of conformity.[23]

THE IDEA OF SERVICE

The idea of service has a long and complex history, and the term has shifted its meaning so much and so often as to be extremely confusing. For long periods, service was either a form of bondage or an aristocratic dedication to the traditional values of agricultural and craft societies. Among the aristocratic elements of such societies, the idea of service carried with it the aura of exclusive privilege and was frequently associated with religious devotion. The very idea of service, in other words, was a polarity of social extremes. In the early period of industrialization, "service" came to have an additional meaning; it became associated with the increasingly large group of very marginal workers in the new industrial centers who could not easily break into the crafts or into industrial manufacturing. These were often "domestic service" workers, and if their political situation was preferable to slaves or serfs, their economic situation was not much better. If we add to this the notion of professional service, once meaning the privileged callings of the clergy, scholarship, and the law but eventually applied to the newer and humbler professional groups of the industrial period, we see at least four, possibly five different meanings of the word.

The professions were not at first well integrated into the new industrial order, for they had too many ties to the disappearing class of aristocratic landowners. This was particularly true for medicine, law, and the clergy, but also for librarianship, at that time really a subfield of scholarship. During this early period of industrialization, the idea of professional service stood in sharp contrast to the idea of profit-making through entrepreneurship. In such circumstances, professionalism could appear, from an ideological standpoint, as a critical force capable of challenging both the dominant ideas of early capitalism and older values of feudal society. In our time the situation is clearly different, since capitalist production has expanded far beyond its origins in manufacturing, and has moved well into the service sector. This "colonization" of service work includes much of what we think of as professional in nature. And this makes it necessary to rethink the idea of service in more modern times—particularly the idea of professional service—for it has been definitively altered in the process.

Thus the twentieth century has seen a shift of its own almost as dramatic as the early development of industrial manufacturing from the economic organizations of feudal Europe. Part of this development is the growth of the service sector of the economy. And part of it is the gradual extension of the capitalist model of production over many areas of service work, gradually absorbing the professions into its orbit. The automation of goods production frees capital to concentrate more resources in investment outside the manufacturing sector. This in turn calls for new groups of workers to fill slots in the expanding service sector. And within the service sector, of course, is where we find a large portion of the information industry.

Clearly the idea of "service" has come a very long way. From a relatively simple opposition between privileged intellectuals and servants of various kinds, it now includes workers of every level of class membership in contemporary society. Somewhere in between these two extremes, the notion of service was useful in distinguishing the genteel work of professionals from the ruggedly competitive struggle of entrepreneurial capitalists. This is a wide and rather confusing range of meanings for one word to carry. What can we learn from this? One lesson is that the idea of "cultivating a service orientation," once thought to be one of the essential distinctions between the professions and business, is now commonly diffused throughout the occupational structure. Even many profit-making occupations claim to serve their publics. Thus unless we understand the term *service* in some way that is specific to contemporary professions, it loses much of its usefulness.

A second lesson is that the older identification between the professions and the service ideal is complicated by remarkable changes in the class structure of advanced industrial societies. "Service" work is now not nearly so low, or so high, as it once was—it is simply one of the major common denominators of modern life. Thus we need to recognize that the drama of "professionalization" so important to many occupations no longer turns on proving that the occupation is organized in the older upper-class style found in the professional work of earlier times. It is rooted in the much larger development of the growth of occupational expertise and the rise of the human services. Professions are no longer automatic tracks leading to the most elite social positions, for contemporary society increasingly reserves these niches for celebrities, business executives, technocrats, and politicians. The overall social meaning of professionalism, in other words, has changed as the society at large has changed, and all this must be taken into account when we try and define what we mean by *service*.

We might, in any case, have wondered at the sharpness of the line between "commercial" and "service" forms of work, since it is relatively easy to dignify the former in the name of the latter. Service clearly can have a ceremonial as well as a descriptive meaning. For these reasons, it is difficult to identify professionalism with any consistent form of service, although one still wants to insist on the importance of the original contrast between attending to client needs and profit making. That surely is of enduring importance. The interdependence of the dimensions of the professionalization process is here underscored, and this is another lesson we can draw from this analysis. By itself, a service orientation, sincere or otherwise, may not be sufficient ground for calling an occupation a profession, but in connection with other traits—the knowledge base, the professional association, the period of formal intellectual training—the case becomes stronger, and the orientation of service appears in a new light.

Librarianship has always been "high" on this trait, relatively untouched by suspicions of commercialism, although this is now possible given recent developments in "information brokering" and "data base management." The key distinction is between the cost-recovery and profit-making versions of these developments. These services are found in libraries, practiced by salaried employees, where they are expected to cover costs, as well as outside the library, practiced by private businesses, where they are expected to earn income above cost. When fees become profits, the offshoot moves away from the professional model and toward business.

We saw in discussing ethics codes the strength of the liberal orientation in librarianship, and this is very much evident in its notion of service. It is rooted in classic liberal social and political theory, which is certainly not the case for all professional groups, particularly the more powerful ones. This ideological position has not helped librarianship to compete against other groups, but it certainly can be read as promoting the needs of users, and in that sense, it is a strong force for professionalization. Besides this, recent public dissatisfaction with paternalism in professional behavior makes librarianship appear, relatively speaking, progressive in its dealings with clients. Until relatively recently a general, almost moral superiority over the client was assumed by many professionals, and this type of superiority is definitely eroding. The erosion reinforces the legitimacy of librarianship's more democratic traditions. This notwithstanding, any claim to professional status must still rest on a superiority of knowledge and training as the common basis of the client's need and the practitioner's ability to serve that need.[24]

SOCIAL RECOGNITION: THE ELUSIVE TRAIT

Most versions of the trait theory reserve a prominent spot for the social recognition that an occupation receives from the surrounding society. Nonetheless, this is extremely hard to measure, and it even may be argued that there is no agreement on how to do it, let alone agreement on which occupations score highest on this trait. Along with the problem of evaluating the knowledge base, it remains perhaps the most difficult problem of the trait theory. Standard indicators of recognition include income, educational attainment of practitioners, prestige of the occupation, degree of autonomy enjoyed by workers, and the prestige of the educational programs. The difficulty is not so much in assessing any of the indicators; the literature of the social and behavioral sciences is full of studies of social and occupational prestige, empirical surveys of professional education, and studies of all kinds drawing reporting correlations between income and prestige, income and autonomy, educational attainment and income, and many more variables. What is hard to do is to draw this into a general measurement of recognition. It is equally difficult to measure, even when taken in isolation, the social influence of a professional association, the recognition of the value and services that professionals provide, and the social standing of the knowledge base.[25]

Is librarianship "low" on social recognition? No doubt this is true in terms of comparative social status and has been since the latter part of the nineteenth century, at least in the United States. But certainly in earlier times librarians had a very exalted status indeed. In the eighteenth and nineteenth centuries the occupation was so prestigious that only major scholars were deemed worthy of entering it. Feminist historians suggest that one of the major reasons for the change was the entry of large numbers of women into the field. In recent years they have quite rightly called attention to "the feminization" of the occupation. This concern has also an interesting variant: it may be not so much the numerical predominance of women, but rather the dominance of a stereotypically feminine image, attached to all librarians, that constitutes the block to recognition. For the sociologically minded, this is a very important and useful point, for the image is at least as important as the fact in understanding questions of power and control.[26]

The feminization thesis is essential for any history of the profession, and is, of course, an important part of the development of American culture generally.[27] It forms one of the central planks in the best of the current work on the history of librarianship, and as such has become an interesting subfield of its own. It is rooted in the feminist insight that rediscovered the centrality of women in maintaining the institutions of our public and elite cultures. Its relevance to the development of librarianship is very obvious, for it is a central historical and sociological fact.

Our focus here, however, is much narrower. In terms of the social recognition of an occupation, there are many factors, usually working simultaneously, operating in the overall development of an occupation that influence the recognition it receives. In engineering and accounting, for example, still predominantly male fields, the narrowness of the knowledge bases, their remoteness from the liberal intellectual culture of the arts and sciences, and the strong emphasis on purely technical competence, have long acted as barriers to social recognition. In occupations based on manual dexterity and physical skill, even where these are highly male-intensive, social recognition will always reflect the fact that the occupations have little or no theoretical content in their knowledge bases. The fact that an occupation is female-intensive may, of course, account for income differentials and perhaps for many differences in occupational prestige, and certainly plays a role in the kind of recognition an occupation receives. But social recognition is only one part of the story of occupational development, and tangible rewards like income and prestige are only part of the story of social recognition. For these reasons the feminization thesis really cannot be used by itself to explain different paths of occupational development. There are too many other factors at work along with it. If this were otherwise, many male-intensive occupations would automatically be much more advanced than they are.

This illustrates a general point that we can use to conclude this chapter, and that is the fact of the interdependence of the traits: the attributes work together to create something called professionalism, or some process called professionalization, but precisely how this occurs remains unclear. As an example of trait interdependence, let us look more closely at the relation between the knowledge base and social recognition.

TRAIT INTERDEPENDENCE

The development of the knowledge base stands in an essential relation to the kind and amount of social recognition that an occupation receives. A highly developed knowledge base with a strong core of theory tends to bring social recognition with it, especially in those cases where the knowledge base is maintained and transmitted by a group of scholars and educators in a university-affiliated professional or graduate school. The reference to theory is essential, for without it the knowledge base is reduced to a set of rules and techniques, and it loses the general intellectual significance that gives it much of its power. Part of the difference between the professional and the nonprofessional lies with the use of theory to situate work in a larger context of liberal learning and a general culture of ideas. And, of course, the identification with the traditions of intellectual culture is one of the major sources of the occupation's recognition as a profession. From this point of view, what distinguishes the work of the librarian from the library technician, the nurse from the nursing assistant, or the lawyer from the paralegal is that the work is grounded in a body of knowledge that has accumulated over a period of time and that is related to leading ideas and findings from some of the major areas of research and scholarship.

This involves some reference to an organized setting where the scholar and the teacher do the work of cultivating the knowledge base and the work of passing it on to new workers; the tasks are too complex and too important to be left to informal processes. Indeed, this is one of the key differences between a craft and a profession. This is what is meant by the "institutionalization" of the professions: that some or all of the work of producing and maintaining the occupation is allotted to some enduring, societywide institution, in this case the institution of education. The general idea of institutionalization is extremely useful in the study of the professions, for it places the traits in a wider context and gives them some social meaning beyond the work of the occupation: there are social functions being fulfilled. Thus it is not only the educational process that is institutionalized, but also the knowledge base, for it is rooted in the life of the professional school, and indirectly in the intellectual traditions of higher education. In Chapter 3, which examines the trait theory critically and introduces alternate approaches, we see that the idea of institutionalization is central to the functionalist theory of the professions.

Recognition comes from other sources as well. To a considerable degree, it comes from a social awareness of the importance of occupational activities. At one time recorded information did not play a particularly significant role in most people's lives; accordingly, librarianship has been for long periods limited in its relevance to a very small sector of the general population. Thus it may once have been possible for most people to simply ignore recorded information and to function largely without formalized systems of information delivery. But it is much more difficult to do this today; and if this is true, public recognition of the importance of all the information occupations will grow along with the social perception of the importance of information. The newer information occupations are on the front edge of the later developments of industrial capitalism; they are growing from within the socioeconomic matrix of the information industry. Since widespread social awareness always lags behind socioeconomic fact, the recognition of the group of occupations also lags behind fact.

NOTES

1. The distinction is suggested by Terence Johnson, *The Professions and Power* (London: Macmillan, 1977), p. 28.
2. The "pure" trait theory can be found in many places, notably Ernest Greenwood, "Attributes of a Profession," *Social Work* 2, 3 (July 1957): 45–55; an application can be found in William J. Goode, "The Librarian: From Occupation to Profession?" *Library Quarterly* 31 (October 1961): 306–20. The "natural history" variant of the trait theory is most clearly illustrated in Harold Wilensky, "The Professionalization of Everyone?"

American Journal of Sociology 70 (September 1964): 137–58, but is also in Theodore Caplow, *The Sociology of Work* (Minneapolis: University of Minnesota Press, 1954), and in Everett C. Hughes, *Men and Their Work* (Glencoe, IL: Free Press, 1958).

3. Wilensky, "The Professionalization of Everyone?" p. 137.

4. Dietrich Rueschemeyer, "Professional Autonomy and the Social Control of Expertise," *The Sociology of the Professions: Lawyers, Doctors, and Others*, eds. Robert Dingwall and Philip Lewis (London: Macmillan, 1983), pp. 45ff.

5. Such deviation is, for the natural history theorist, an indication of partial professionalization. Wilensky, "Professionalization of Everyone?" p. 144.

6. Ibid., p. 145.

7. Autonomy is given a central position by Wilbert Moore in *The Professions: Roles and Rules* (New York: Sage, 1970). The idea of a "professional culture" is discussed by Greenwood, "Attributes of a Profession," p. 45. Other traits are distributed widely and more or less evenly throughout the literature on the professions.

8. Wilensky, "Professionalization of Everyone?" p. 143.

9. The relation between social distance and indeterminacy is suggested by Dietrich Rueschemeyer, "Doctors and Lawyers: A Comment on the Theory of the Professions," *Canadian Journal of Sociology and Anthropology* 1 (February 1964): 17–30, but it is implicit in many discussions.

10. Marcia J. Bates, "Rigorous Systematic Bibliography," *RQ* 16 (Fall 1976): 7–26. The argument is partly based on Patrick Wilson's *Two Kinds of Power: An Essay on Bibliographic Control* (Berkeley: University of California Press, 1968).

11. Daniel Patrick Moynihan, a sociologist and senior official in the Department of Labor, was the principal investigator for *The Negro Family: The Case for National Action*, Office of Policy Planning and Research, U.S. Department of Labor (Washington, DC: GPO, 1965). Two social scientists who had significant influence on the Supreme Court decision are Kenneth Clark and Robert Redfield, but many others were involved. See Richard Kluger, *Simple Justice: The History of Brown v. Board of Education and Black America's Struggle for Equality* (New York: Knopf, 1976), pp. 129–30, 265, 315–19, 422.

12. Patrick Wilson, "Bibliographical R & D," *The Study of Information: Interdisciplinary Messages*, eds. Fritz Machlup and Una Mansfield (New York: Wiley, 1983), p. 390.

13. The evidence for this claim, based on a recent study, is provided in Chapter 6.

14. Some of the philosophical background of the rise of the professions in relation to liberal thought is supplied by Alfred North Whitehead, *Adventures of Ideas* (New York: Free Press, 1967), pp. 57–62. We know, of course, that professional autonomy is limited by material factors also, by social, economic, and political forces outside the occupation (discussed in Chapter 3).

15. Paul Wasserman, *The New Librarianship: Challenge for Change* (New York: R. R. Bowker, 1972).

16. There is a useful historical sketch of the association in A. M. Carr-Saunders and P. A. Wilson, *The Professions* (London: Cass, 1964), pp. 298–304.

17. At one time this included physicians. Carr-Saunders and Wilson, p. 298.

18. Ibid., pp. 298ff.

19. Ibid., p. 300.

20. Professionals in the early modern period were acutely conscious of the need to raise their social status. Carr-Saunders and Wilson, pp. 302–3.

21. Thus Robert T. Bower and Priscilla de Gasparis report that at least thirty-nine professional associations are without formal ethics codes, including the American Association of Social Psychiatry, the American Society of Human Genetics, and the American Statistical Association. See *Ethics and Social Research: Protecting the Interests of Human Subjects* (New York: Praeger, 1978).

22. William J. Goode, "Encroachment, Charlatanism, and the Emerging Profession: Psychology, Sociology, and Medicine," *American Sociological Review* 25 (December 1960): 902–14.

23. I allude to the distinction between normative and structural control drawn by William J. Reeves in *Librarians as Professionals: The Occupation's Impact on Library Work Arrangements* (Lexington, MA: D. C. Heath, 1980), pp. xix-xx, 11–115, 133–34. This point is elaborated in Chapter 4.

24. Librarianship's liberalism may stem from the fact that the occupation is relatively more recent as a full-time pursuit than either law or medicine, which are both rooted in much older traditions. For example, medicine's concern with health can be traced to early Greek philosophy: Werner Jaeger, *Paideia: The Ideals of Greek Culture*, vol. III, trans. Gilbert Highet (New York: Oxford University Press, 1945), pp. 3–44. The concept of justice has a similarly ancient heritage in Egyptian and Greek mythology. By contrast, the notions of toleration, freedom of access, and such are relatively new ideas, products of an enlightenment synthesis. A pure form of this liberal idealism can be found in David Berninghausen, *The Flight from Reason: Essays in Intellectual Freedom in the Academy, the Press, and the Library* (Chicago: American Library Association, 1975).

25. Studies of occupational prestige were at one time so common that one writer was led to observe that they had become part of the core of the sociology of the professions. Everett C. Hughes, *The Sociological Eye* (New Brunswick, NJ: Transaction Books, 1985), p. 366. These studies are not nearly so common today.

26. On feminization, see Dee Garrison, "The Tender Technicians: Feminization of Public Librarianship, 1876–1905," *Journal of Social History* 6 (Winter 1972–73): 131–58; by the same author, *Apostles of Culture: The Public Librarian and American Society, 1876–1920* (New York: Free Press, 1979), pp. 173–85, 235–38, 241; and Jody Newmeyer, "The Image Problem of the Librarian: Femininity and Social Control," *Journal of Library History* 11 (January, 1976): 44–67. For examples of additional work in this area, see among others, Suzanne Hildenbrand, "Some Theoretical Considerations on Women in Library History," *Journal of Library History, Philosophy, and Comparative Librarianship* 18, 4 (Fall 1983): 382–90; and Barbara Brand, "Librarianship and Other Female-Intensive Professions," *Journal of Library History, Philosophy, and Comparative Librarianship* 18, 4 (Fall 1983): 391–406. Comparative and historical methods are united in Mary Niles Maack, "Women Librarians in France: The First Generation," *Journal of Library History, Philosophy, and Comparative Librarianship* 18, 4 (Fall 1983): 407–49. For a useful anthology, see Kathleen M. Heim, ed., *Women in Librarianship* (New York: Neal-Schuman, 1983).

27. Ann Douglas, *The Feminization of American Culture* (New York: Knopf, 1977).

3

Differentiation and Contrast: Functionalist and Occupational Control Theories of the Professions

The view of professions and professionalization discussed in Chapter 2 as the trait theory is typical of much twentieth-century thinking. For many writers the trait approach is, theoretically speaking, the end of the story, and the real work of understanding professionalization begins with its application to specific examples. This was partly true even in sociology, where the study of the professions has reached its most sophisticated expression, at least until functionalist theory arrived in the 1940s and 1950s to provide an alternative.

There are numerous classic examples of the trait theory in operation in sociology as well as in the professional literature of librarianship.[1] A few key examples can demonstrate the strength of its influence in library literature. In the 1950s Pierce Butler assumed a relatively straightforward model of the trait theory.[2] This is not surprising, since the functionalist challenge had only just begun to materialize at about that time. What is more noteworthy is that the trait theory persists, almost untouched by reflective criticism, in library literature up to the present. In addition to works already cited, it appears in the early 1960s, the mid- and late 1970s, and again in 1980. It is ubiquitous.[3] In almost all library literature that is related in some way to the sociological study of the professions, the trait approach is dominant.[4]

CRITIQUE OF THE TRAIT THEORY: CONCEPT AND METHOD

As we have seen, the trait theory assumes that professions are types of occupations possessing certain qualities, and that "professionalization" is the process of acquiring those qualities. In the natural history variant, the qualities are acquired in sequential order; this sequence is crucial to "professionalization," and thus to determining how highly "professionalized" a given occupation is. These ideas are part of the conceptual framework presupposed by the trait approach.

But in addition to a conceptual framework, the trait theory has a distinctive methodological framework: a set of ideas and assumptions guiding empirical investigation. For example, the trait approach assumes that the possession of an attribute, and the degree of completeness with which it is possessed, can be measured. The natural history variant makes another assumption: that we can track the sequence of acquiring the traits and thus construct empirically verifiable indicators of how highly professionalized an occupation is, meaning that occupations can be ranked on scales showing attribute possession and sequences of acquisition.

When we look at individual traits, however, we really see a mixed picture; some are relatively easy to measure, but in others the very idea of measurement seems almost incoherent. In addition, it is very difficult to understand how an overall ranking that represents all the attributes could be produced. For instance, we can certainly measure the presence or absence of a university program, or the number of years between the founding of an occupation and the establishment of its university schools. We might rate occupations on the presence or absence of an association, and we could count the number of years between the founding of the occupation and the birth of the association. And these types of measures could be used with ethics codes as well. But when we look at the knowledge base, for example, or the service orientation or social recognition, the picture is much more complex. Each of these traits is really a complex, multidimensional cluster rather than a single trait, and although we might define each dimension carefully enough to permit measurement, how would we then draw all the scores together into a composite picture of the trait as a whole? The fact is that we cannot really do this, because the different dimensions of each trait are too heterogeneous to permit a summary score that represents any occupation's degree of "professionalization" on a given multidimensional trait. Suppose, for example, that the knowledge base of one occupation is high on the quality of its scientific literature, medium on the amount of useful theory it generates, and low on the degree of difficulty for outsiders to master. Another occupation has a very esoteric knowledge base, not much theoretical development, and a literature of medium quality. Even assuming we can produce satisfactory measurements of each element in the cluster, how do we add them up to produce an overall assessment of the knowledge base? And would this be useful? On conceptual grounds alone, the answers to these questions tell us that the attempt to measure professionalization in this way is at least very difficult and at most not very useful.

This is not to say that, given enough expertise and attention, methodological solutions could not be produced. But though it may be possible in principle, the trait theory faces an even greater problem. The problem is in its conceptual framework, something that is not amenable to methodological tinkering.

Conceptually speaking, the trait theory is based on a fatal flaw in attempting to define its key terms. Since theory precedes method when evaluating the overall value of an intellectual strategy, let us look at this more closely. The problem is not so much in the way the terms are defined, but in the idea of definition underlying the theory. We can call this underlying notion the assumption of "essential definition." It is based on the idea that a term has a straightforward relationship to some fact in the world or to some state of affairs, and that this relationship gives a term its essential meaning.

The essence of water, let us say, is a certain combination of hydrogen and oxygen at certain temperatures. Most of us are familiar with this seemingly uncomplicated definition, even though we have many other informal working definitions that are much more relevant to us in ordinary affairs. ("Water is what we drink," "water is what we wash clothes in," and so on.) The definition of the term *water* is provided by pointing to certain facts that give us the essential characteristics of the substance—two atoms of hydrogen, one of oxygen, above freezing and below evaporation temperatures. The problem is that the "pointing" relationship leaves out a whole world of context. The word *water*, defined chemically, is meaningful only if one knows what hydrogen and oxygen are; but millions of people know perfectly well what water is without knowing anything of these "essential" attributes. In understanding definition, context is all; and it is only in certain highly specialized contexts, such as natural science, that context can be suppressed. And if this is true, the whole idea of defining a term by telling what it "points" to is not an adequate form of definition. It is only a way of defining a term for certain limited purposes.

Even with this qualification, the assumption of essential definition only works adequately with very simple terms. Thus, while it may be possible to specify certain contexts in which water is defined as "one atom of oxygen and two of hydrogen, between certain temperatures," it cannot be done with a term of any complexity. The reason, again, is context: the meaning of a term has much more to do with the context in which it is found than in its relationship to a set of attributes or traits. From this viewpoint, the trait approach to the professions appears to be based, at least implicitly, on a rather simplistic notion of definition, and this is its greatest problem. Or, we can say that the trait theory is just too naive and too hasty in its attempt to define what "profession" means. Or, we might say that although the trait theory works to a certain point, it runs into difficulty rather quickly. However, as long as we realize this, there is no reason why we cannot use it up to that point. When the user begins to take the limited definition as an indisputable basis of a comprehensive theory, however, we are justified in asking for something more sophisticated.[5]

A simple illustration, akin to the problem in defining water, is found in the observation that the term profession has certain connotations that vary broadly by culture. In Anglo-American usage, profession usually excludes the kind of craft labor found in highly skilled working-class occupations because it is enmeshed in a certain set of social distinctions. In French and German, on the other hand, the terms *profession* and *Beruf* may designate any full-time occupation pursued as a career. Our concern here is mainly with the professions as they have developed in Anglo-American tradition, in which *profession* generally refers to certain middle-class occupations, but it should be remembered that a term is not defined by only one of its uses.[6]

The view of definition outlined here is basically pragmatic and social. It follows everyday usage and does not specify once and for all the meanings of terms by providing lists of attributes. The pragmatic view looks rather at how a term functions in different contexts and sees "meaning" as a kind of summary of how the word has been or is currently being used. Linguistically speaking, we have a practical definition: asking what a term means is asking how certain communities of persons actually use the term, and this may involve reference to a large number of activities. One of the more interesting consequences of this view of language is that it points us in the direction of social activity, and we begin to see language as one aspect of social life, subject to regulation by shared standards of conduct. For this among other reasons, we find that alternatives to the trait theory began to surface at about the same time that the functionalist paradigm of social life appeared.

THE EMERGENCE OF FUNCTIONALISM

In contrast to the trait theory, the functionalist approach holds that professionalization is not primarily a matter of acquiring attributes but rather is a process by which certain occupations come to play particular kinds of social roles. More narrowly, it looks to the professional-client relationship as a central problem.[7] There is, nevertheless, some overlap between trait and functionalist approaches, since the "functional characteristics" of professions are clearly related to what we find on trait lists. Talcott Parsons, for example, specifies three crucial functional characteristics: formal training in a field whose core is a cognitive discipline (as opposed to a technical, practical, or primarily intuitive discipline); development of skills related to this knowledge; and an institutional framework controlling the applications of these skills.[8]

The general relationship between the trait and functionalist approaches is illustrated in Figure 3–1.

Despite the verbal similarity between "characteristics" and "traits," functionalism does something rather different with its analysis: professions are seen as types of occupations that play a certain role in maintaining the overall equilibrium of the social system, by providing for certain fundamental social needs. The trait approach, by comparison, is an attempt to paint on a rather small canvas, while functionalism is trying to produce a mural with a place on it for professions. For the functionalist synthesis, the study of the professions is only one aspect of the great problem of maintaining the social balance. It is rooted in the philosophical encounter with Darwinism in the mid-nineteenth century, and rests on an analogy between society and the biological organism. Its major insight is expressed by the attempt to replace the static with the dynamic in the

Figure 3–1
Comparison of Trait and Functionalist Models

Trait Model	Functionalist Model
Professional Association	Institutionalization
Professional School	.of professional training
	.of knowledge base
Knowledge Base	
	.control over professional
Other Traits	knowledge

study of social structure: societies, like animals, are adaptive creatures attempting to reduce uncertainty and powerlessness in the face of nature.[9]

Of the many meanings attached to the idea of "function" in sociology, we may single out two as especially relevant here: function is tied to "appropriate activity," and it is expressed in the central relation of reciprocity; it is "system determined and system determining." Functionalism early on divided into two great branches: a broad general level of analysis that concentrates on the most abstract levels of social structure (macrofunctionalism), and an interactional level, where the units of analysis are individual persons, interpersonal relationships, and small groups.[10] The two levels work together in the "system determined and system determining" symbiosis of parts and wholes: social structures provide the large-scale stability of social action over longer periods of time; small groups and face-to-face interactions, on the other hand, provide the most immediately experienced context of social life. In this ambitious program, there is a place for everything that is social; a place for institutions, organizations, and patterns of social structure that stretch across whole societies, and a place for the intimate give-and-take of ordinary social life.

The bridge between functionalism as a general theory of social life and its theory of the professions is the concept of institutionalization. "Maintaining the social balance" turns out to be primarily a matter of providing a regular reasonably efficient means for dealing with the most basic problems of social life. Thus, to assure the supply of food and shelter, we have a patterned network of social activity, which we call the "economy"; to provide some kind of social control, usually in the form of government and the law, we have an even more carefully patterned network, which we call "politics." Similarly, we have the family for the control of sexual life and reproduction, religion for spiritual needs, and, to guarantee an acceptable level of knowledge in the citizenry, the institution of education. A social institution, in this view, is an overlapping pattern of social activities with a common function, and as a pattern "hardens," the institution becomes more established in its roles.[11] Professions are types of occupations designed to provide certain essential services, and the provision of these services requires a substantial period of higher learning. The professions, in other words, are "institutionalized" by being situated in the much larger patterned network of education, and, more exactly, in that part of the network discharging the functions of higher education.

CONCEPTUAL AND HISTORICAL CRITIQUE: THE CONTROL MODEL

As we have seen, there is some overlap between the trait and functionalist views, even though they are clearly different approaches. It could be said that the point of overlap is in a key shared assumption: professions are types of occupations. This assumption seems so obvious that one can hardly imagine how it could be criticized. How could a profession be anything *but* a type of occupation? And yet it is this precise notion that has been subjected to a thorough and very convincing critique in recent years, as an entirely new approach to the study of the professions has emerged. One of the first sociologists to strike out in this direction was Terence Johnson, who argued that both the trait theory and the functionalist view of professions suffer from this assumption and they fail to grasp important points as a result. In particular, Johnson argues that both approaches lack historical perspective and in effect give us oversimplified cross sections of professions as they are at certain times and under certain conditions, but no more.[12]

This historical critique is serious, but Johnson also argues that the very idea of a profession as a type of occupation is a fundamental conceptual confusion: a profession, he suggests, is not at all a kind of occupation, but rather a complex set of procedures for controlling an occupation. Much of the same could be said of union or guild, since they are all attempts to control certain types of work routines. And this is very different. This criticism is tantamount to saying that *profession* and *occupation* are not even members of the same general class.[13] It may be useful here to review some of the background of this criticism and provide some illustrations of its power.

The idea is that the term *profession* belongs with the closely related terms of *union*, *guild*, and other forms of control rather than with terms naming occupational groups. In this context, it would be confusing to say that law, medicine, and librarianship are professions, just as it would be confusing to say that plumbing is a union or that clockmaking is a guild. Rather we should say that law and librarianship are "professionalized occupations," just as we should say that plumbing is a unionized occupation and that clockmaking is a craft-organized occupation. Law, medicine, librarianship, clockmaking, and plumbing are *all* occupations; where they differ is in the types of control they exhibit. The difference is between occupations that rely on advanced degrees and intellectual credentials, and those that rely on manual dexterity and skills generally acquired during work-based apprenticeships. Law, medicine, and librarianship tend toward the professional model of control; clockmaking and plumbing show forms of control found in skilled working-class occupations.

People who assume that a profession is a certain kind of occupation express this confusion because they assume that *profession* and *occupation* refer to objects in the same general class of things. But if a profession is a type of control, then it is in a different class altogether. And if we are going to understand "professions," then we must turn to the study of mechanisms of control. Trait theorists and functionalists could argue that the criticism does not apply because they are trying to understand how professional workers exercise control, and they accomplish this by developing knowledge bases, codes of ethics, university programs, institutional frameworks, and so on. And this may be true, but one can see already that this involves a major concession to Johnson's concern with control. And, in fact, this reply would be only partly convincing, since trait theorists and functionalists alike have, at least in some measure, neglected the question of control.

The matter of control is what brings us to Johnson's historical critique. By not looking closely at actual examples of occupations and by looking at only a few occupations as they exist under contemporary conditions, the sociology of the professions has in effect eliminated the historical dimension. This produces a skewed analysis. The trait theory does this quite naively—by simply ignoring history, functionalism does it because it is too eager to construct its general theory of society and too eager to place professions within that general theory.[14] One consequence is that the functionalist theory tends to ignore a whole range of phenomena, particularly in the area of social conflict. Focusing on the balance struck in the social system as a whole, it glosses over details.

Based on these and related criticisms, Johnson and other writers developed a three-part model of occupational control. In collegial control, producers define consumer needs and the best manner of meeting them, and they typically rely on fellow professionals for help when problems arise. This type of occupational control, says Johnson, has usually been called "professionalism." In the second type, client control, users of services define both their own needs and the manner of addressing them. Mediated control is a hybrid type in which the intervention of some powerful third party, such as a government agency, or an abstract socioeconomic force, such as the marketplace, qualifies the relationship between the producers and users of professional services. Johnson also argues that mediated control is the general direction in which almost all occupations, including the collegially controlled ones, are heading. Collegial control has certainly not disappeared, but the mixed type is rising in importance.

Let us look at some examples. In collegial control, a librarian decides, based on a user's statements and questions, that a need for a certain type of information is being expressed, perhaps incompletely or incorrectly, recommends a source on that basis, and evaluates the quality of the source in that context. This is analogous to a physician who diagnoses a patient and then uses the diagnosis to develop a treatment strategy. The physician, like the librarian, may consult a colleague in the process. Or, in another example, a librarian, who decides that a certain group of users is ill-served by one type of classification scheme, constructs or adopts another, or modifies the current one. In client control, a patient tells a physician that she has the flu, asks for a specific drug, and the physician writes the prescription. A library user decides that he needs *Statistical Abstracts of the United States*, and the librarian finds the source. Mediating factors, as we have seen, can be clients or client-based organizations, social agencies (government or legislative bodies and their policies), abstract social forces, general social trends (such as the development of automation), changes in cultural orientations and values, and others. For example, a head librarian at a public library finds that citizens' groups seek to influence the library's acquisitions policy (perhaps to impose certain moral values); a cataloger finds that the tasks of original cataloging are altered by the use of bibliographic utilities. A lawyer finds that the most successful of her colleagues rely on consultants whose authority is based on the expertise of a variety of nonlegal occupations (such as quantitative analysis of jury selection processes). And in all these cases, everyone finds that the work is increasingly dependent on high technology, the corporate invasion of professional labor markets, and a new urgency in the need to protect client privacy.

A REORIENTATION OF RESEARCH

The above examples look at professional work from the standpoint of type of control exercised, and do not make specific reference to traits or to any of the underlying institutional considerations noted earlier. The stress is on who is directing the delivery of the service. This new approach clearly calls for a reorientation of research and interpretation. Focused historical analyses of occupations, relationships between occupations, their clienteles, and any mediating forces replace the attempt to develop lists of attributes or functional characteristics.[15]

One important consequence of this is the blurring of the distinction between *occupation* and *profession*, for when we look closely we find that no occupation is ever purely collegially controlled, and also because we can approach the study of any occupation by looking at mechanisms of control. Of course, it is still possible to distinguish between collegially controlled occupations whose expertise is intellectual, as opposed to those where client control dominates, or those with the mediated form, or, again, those whose expertise is based on mastery of craft lore, physical skill, manual dexterity, or specialized manual technique. Indeed, with the occupational control approach, we can make a great many rather fine distinctions in producing a typology of professional groups. But we no longer have any clear-cut, quick method of separating professions from occupations.

But although the thinking represented by Johnson and others is very plausible and although they are surely right in maintaining that no theory of the professions can continue to use the older approaches without modification, it would be a mistake to conclude that the trait and functionalist approaches have no value at all. It is true that no occupation has ever been purely collegially or professionally controlled and that numerous challenges to professional authority have undermined some of the authority of even the strongest and most entrenched occupational groups.[16] Even so, many of the occupations that do show a high degree of control over their own work routines and over general definitions of service are the same ones identified by the earlier views as highly professionalized.[17] Further, even if we find the trait and functionalist approaches to be theoretically inadequate from certain viewpoints, professionalization remains at least partly a process of social definition. Thus to the extent that traits and functional characteristics are *thought* to be important, they *are* important, because public recognition of an occupation's activities is a central fact of its position in the social structure.[18]

RETHINKING AUTONOMY

In another way, the turn toward occupational control reflects the relevance of the earlier approaches; for autonomy and control, although not the same, are closely related. And autonomy has sometimes been seen as a central feature by trait and functionalist writers alike.[19] But its most precise analysis has come from the more recent approaches. Friedson, for example, introduces the idea of "zones of autonomy" and distinguishes between "technical" (or "specific") autonomy in routine work and "general" autonomy or the broader control over the socioeconomic organization of the work process. Also in the zone of general autonomy are found problems in the general definition of service and the clarification of values. Thus when we speak of "occupational control," we are speaking of two different types of autonomous action: control over special techniques of delivery and control over the broad goals of the profession. Although Freidson regards the technical zone as the most crucial to the maintenance of collegial or professional control, in the long run the two zones are probably interdependent.[20]

The concept of autonomy is perhaps one of the central threads in all the approaches to the study of the professions. But though it is a common element, the interpretation shifts depending on the theory. The approach to autonomy in the trait and functionalist views is generally collegial in a very strong sense, as if no mediated forms were possible. In the occupational control approach, autonomy has two interpretations: collegial and mediated, with the line between the two not at all easy to draw in real cases. (Pure forms of client control do not appear to be very widely distributed.) Certain occupations show many instances of basically collegial control, with some mediating factors. Lawyers working in collectively managed law firms, or physicians in private forms of group practice, for example, contend with trends in office automation, dependence on outside consultants to use new technologies, and a shifting labor market for legal and medical services. The same can be said for many types of librarians: autonomous control is qualified by certain forces but generally not by powerful clients or external bureaucracies. But other types of lawyers and physicians, and other types of librarians, experience much greater degrees of mediation. Some special and academic librarians have virtually no authority over selection and other aspects of collection development, but do have complete authority over acquisitions and other functions. In this situation autonomy is confined—to use Freidson's distinction—to the technical zone. Lawyers in corporate settings are much more toward the client control end of the spectrum, while physicians employed in health care organizations experience relatively high degrees of mediation from their employers, but generally not from their patients. What all this suggests is that collegial control tends to increase with the prevalence of "group practice" as opposed to practice in some setting populated with and controlled by workers of some other occupation.

The Knowledge Base and Autonomy

There is a close connection between the analysis of autonomy and the nature of the knowledge base upon which professional practice is founded. As this knowledge tends toward the technical, its mastery becomes progressively easier to reduce to sets of rules. We might say that it has, in this case, a "determinate" quality. This has two crucial consequences for professionalization. First, it makes the knowledge base relatively easier to master; second, it makes it easier for an occupation to be controlled by some external force. On the other hand, as the knowledge base becomes more theoretical, and more indeterminate, its basic principles are harder to reduce to rules, and its general accessibility diminishes, rendering control from outside more difficult. Clearly, indeterminacy in the knowledge base favors the collegial form of control, while technicality favors either client control or a higher level of mediation.[21]

We saw that in the trait theory there is an important relationship between knowledge and autonomy.[22] This is also true in the occupational control approach, but the focus is somewhat different. The newer approach places knowledge in relation to the two zones, seeing the zones as contributing to varying degrees of control over practice. Thus the technical part of the knowledge base (for example, selection, acquisitions, cataloging, the book trade, systems and automation) is most closely related to maintaining control in the narrower zone, while the more theoretical parts of the knowledge base (theory of classification and indexing, theory of intellectual freedom, social and behavioral analysis of user needs and user behavior, study of the characteristics of bodies of literature and collections) is most closely related to the general zone. To the extent that one zone is cultivated over others, there will be imbalances in the development of the knowledge base that will have strong effects on professional practice. The point here is that one is looking at the knowledge base in terms of its value for control.

A MARXIST THEORY OF THE PROFESSIONS

The idea of a reorientation of research has proved influential, and there are at present a number of writers studying occupational control. In his earlier work Johnson argued that professional or collegial control over work develops only under certain conditions: the existence of a large, urban middle class, recruitment of workers from middle-class and upper-middle-class backgrounds, and a homogeneous occupational community.[23] In a later development Johnson turns to a more specialized type of the control approach and builds a Marxist model of occupations, arguing that professional control exists only where it is not in the interests of capital to organize the work process in the interests of profit and corporate control. Types of work that escape the profit-seeking long arm of capitalism, in other words, will be freer to develop the collegial pattern.[24] Some recent trends in librarianship do suggest increased involvement in profit making, but on the whole the field is still not particularly attractive to corporate investment. Nonetheless this point of view is interesting because the traditional remoteness of librarians from the production and distribution of commodities is clearly changing; and for certain types of information workers—for example, special librarians and documentation specialists in corporate settings—the problem of corporate control is a very real one.

We need not be concerned with the forbidding details of the Marxist analysis of advanced industrial society, but the general insight that capital in its search for new markets tends to "colonize" labor markets is very significant for understanding professionalization in our time. The connection between capitalism and industrial society is so strong that we may forget that capital can and does accumulate almost anywhere that profit is to be made. Looked at historically, the slow accumulation and concentration of capital began by affecting only a few sectors of the economy, mainly the production of hard goods. As the processes continued, more and more sectors were absorbed; theoretically, any part of economic life can be subjected to their control. At a certain point capital finds a saturated market in goods production and begins to move outward into newer areas of enterprise—into services, including professional services. At first it moves into service industries without much collegial control, but there is now evidence that it is taking over traditional professional services such as law and medicine.[25] One consequence is a considerable loss of collegial control in favor of corporate control.[26]

ARE PROFESSIONS LOSING GROUND? THE DEPROFESSIONALIZATION THESIS

The more recent literature on the professions, as we have seen, departs from trait and functionalist approaches in a number of ways. It rejects many of the

theoretical and methodological assumptions of both, and it suggests some problems with a purely functional approach to occupations that ignores concrete
factors in historical development. In focusing on power and control as central
issues, it recognizes the fact that the growth of the professions cannot be under-
stood outside the context of the struggle for dominance. And perhaps most
significantly, it interprets "control" in two different ways: the ways in which
occupations control themselves and attempt to control the delivery of services,
and the ways in which they may come to be controlled by outside forces. We
saw, in discussing the emergence of a Marxist theory of professions, the idea
of corporate control. When we look at the larger picture, we see that this is only
one kind of "external" threat to autonomy; there are others. And this fact has
led to what may be seen as a particularly radical version of the control approach,
which suggests that there is a backward movement in the professionalization
process—a reversal of professionalization, or a movement of "deprofessionalization."

Is professional freedom receding, advancing, or staying the same? This much
asked question is very hard to answer. The reason lies in what Everett Hughes
has called "the paradox of professional freedom."[27] On the one hand, a number
of trends appear to limit professional freedom, among them the advance of
bureaucracy, the fact that almost all work is now situated in very complex
organizations, the development of new technologies (particularly automation),
and competition from newer occupations. At the same time these developments
make possible a great expansion of professional services, and thus create new
markets for delivery. In so doing they increase the professional's freedom by
providing new opportunities for practice.

An example can be found in professional-client relations. The demand for
services assumes a general level of knowledge, even sophistication, among users
of services. Without an increasing level of such knowledge among clients, it
would be difficult for professional markets to expand. On the other hand, such
sophistication also promotes a greater skepticism toward professional authority.
This general insight is the basis of what some recent writers see as a movement
of deprofessionalization, or loss of control.[28] Haug, for example, points to the
importance of computers as one specific factor that undermines the older idea
of professional control of the knowledge base; and the emergence of large numbers of computer experts to use and maintain these utilities further threatens the
professional's autonomy in the delivery of services.[29]

This is an important challenge in libraries, where current staffing reflects
significant involvement of these new types of workers and their expertise. Another example comes from organizational management, and a similar point may
be made in regard to managerial and administrative roles in libraries, which
further detract from the librarian's ability to concentrate exclusively on professional work.[30] In this case, the growth and development of the occupation itself
triggers a differentiation within itself, splitting off a new occupational type, even
though most library administrators come from the ranks of professional workers.

These challenges come from outside the routine tasks of the occupation and the professional-client relationship in a narrow sense; they arise from the fact that work organizations in their complexity frequently contain more than one type of occupation, and because authority may be assumed by workers from other fields or by workers who have in effect moved into a new occupational group.

Deprofessionalization has an interesting analogue in working-class occupations, suggesting the possibility of an important general trend in work. Marxian thinkers have for some time pointed to the gradual erosion of skill or craft in the core areas of manufacturing, and have more recently argued that this has spread to all areas of work in contemporary society—the "degradation of work," as it has been called.[31] The focus of this analysis has been in the working-class occupations, but it seems clear that the general drift of the deprofessionalization thesis applies to middle-class occupations as well, and this includes the professionally controlled ones.

Naturally we cannot deal exhaustively with these large problems here, but we can use them as background for asking some analytical questions about the organization of work in librarianship. One of the first questions concerns how librarianship has responded to the coexistence of different occupational types within library organizations. Unfortunately not much work has examined this problem, but an important recent empirical study is relevant. Despite the presence of different occupational types in the library organization, it is still librarians who define, by their occupational orientations toward library associations and the library schools, their work and the manner in which it is to be carried out.[32]

What can be said about the effect of computerization? Here the available evidence is even slimmer, but some data indicate that the effects of automation are subtle and complex. This much is clear: computerization seems to have two major effects. It complicates the occupational structure of the organization by bringing in new types of workers, and it dramatically alters the nature of the labor process. To the degree that automation carries the division of labor further than ever before, it redefines many tasks once thought to be unambiguously professional. These tasks are then transferred to paraprofessionals or clerical workers. Examples abound in acquisitions and cataloging, where the ratio of professional to nonprofessional workers has greatly declined in recent years. The difficult question raised here is whether there is really a *qualitative* alteration of the task: has the job really changed or has its manner of execution been changed? If automation does not qualitatively transform work, it can make some tasks so relatively simple that it no longer makes sense to have professionals do them. In this sense, some technical services functions have certainly been deprofessionalized. But at the same time the supervisory function of the professional is probably much more challenging, since it now requires a broader view of the labor process.[33]

In public services the major force has been the coming of online searching, which presents a very different situation. A good case has been made that online searching actually enhances the professional function, and thus has an effect precisely opposite to what the deprofessionalization thesis suggests. Nielsen argues that the use of computers in information retrieval has a number of professionalizing effects: increased complexity of interaction with users, encouragement of greater subject specialization, separation of data base searching from paraprofessional reference work, and increased control over interaction with users. In most of these we see the model of collegial control.[34] Naturally this will be more true where search techniques are relatively complex and require extended periods of learning to apply, and, of course, one of the main trends in the information industry is to simplify access to put it within reach of the average consumer. If this trend continues and "end-user searching" becomes widespread, the deprofessionalization thesis will seem more plausible.

But even this would not be conclusive evidence for deprofessionalization, for one of the consequences of end-user searching might well be an increased demand for the more complex mediated searching that requires the services of the professional. These developments are far too new to gauge their impact, but on logical grounds the argument is quite easy to follow. The end users will quickly discover, once they have experimented with the simpler search strategies, that there are things they cannot make the system do, and they will turn to professionals for help. In this very plausible scenario, users take control over task areas just as they are being replaced by more advanced methods, and the professional assumes the role of the specialized consultant.

Deprofessionalization or Mediation?

How do we thread our path through all this? Without giving a definitive answer, we can at least simplify it. The question of whether or not we are being deprofessionalized can be seen as a more specific question: how do we interpret challenges to collegial control? In a sense we have one set of phenomena that can be viewed in different ways. One view looks at all these challenges as a token of backward movement. But one might also argue, following Johnson's three-level model, that the consequence of challenge to professional authority is not something called "deprofessionalization," but rather the gradual coming of mediated control.[35] The deprofessionalization thesis plausibly isolates challenges to the absolute power of professional groups, but then the very idea of complete control as the basis of professional power is itself rather questionable. Occupational control has probably never been absolute and has always been checked to some degree by intervening forces.

Bureaucracy and Occupational Control

We have seen that technological developments are paralleled by changes in modes of organization and have noted that bureaucratic organization challenges professional control. The earlier work on professionalization pointed to a basic opposition between professionalism and bureaucracy—it tends to pit professionals against bureaucracies. The more recent work has some rather different implications for the whole question of bureaucracy. The reason is that bureaucratic organization is now so widespread that it cannot simply be identified with managerial authority; all work, to a greater or lesser degree, is organized along bureaucratic lines, even when it is not dominated by managers. The impulse to bureaucratize can and does flow from sources within occupations. In these cases, it is a reflection of the collective will of the group—and expression rather than a limitation of autonomy. The growth of an occupation by itself brings about a need for coordination of specialized areas of practice; changing definitions of professional work reflect also a greater emphasis on teamwork or in larger groups than in working by oneself; and increased reliance on complex technologies introduces more complex problems of many kinds whose solutions strongly encourage bureaucratization. The lawyer who does not use computerized indexes to case law cannot keep up; the physician ignorant of nuclear medicine and computerized diagnosis cannot practice state-of-the-art medicine; and the librarian who does not use automated retrieval techniques cannot provide the services that many users now need. From this point of view, the bureaucratically structured organizations we work in are not forced upon us; they are consequences of the way we do our work. Of course, there will always be bureaucratic forces that do not flow from our own definitions of work, and, of course, *these* forces are mediating forces, to return once again to Johnson's model.

NOTES

1. From sociology, for example, William J. Goode, "The Librarian: From Occupation to Profession?" *Library Quarterly* 31 (October 1961): 306–20; Harold Wilensky, "The Professionalization of Everyone?" *American Journal of Sociology* 70 (September 1964): 143ff.; and Ernest Greenwood, "Attributes of a Profession," *Social Work* 2, 3 (July 1957): 45–55. There are a great many others.

2. Pierce Butler, "Librarianship as a Profession," *Library Quarterly* 21, 4 (October 1951): 245ff.

3. For example, Philip Ennis, ed., *Seven Questions About the Profession of Librarianship* (Chicago: University of Chicago Press, 1961); John North, "Librarianship: Profession?" *Canadian Library Journal* 34, 4 (April 1977): 253–57; Kathleen M. Heim, "Professional Education: Some Comparisons," *As Much to Learn as to Teach: Essays in Honor of Lester Asheim*, eds. J. M. Lee and B. A. Hamilton (Hamden, CT: Linnet Books, 1979), pp. 128–76; David G. E. Sparks, "Academic Librarianship: Professional Strivings and Political Realities," *College and Research Libraries* 41, 5 (September 1980): 408–21. These are a very small sample.

4. The exceptions are works that deal with librarianship as a profession without looking specifically to sociological models for inspriation, for example, Mary Lee Bundy and Paul Wasserman, "Professionalism Reconsidered," *College and Research Libraries* 29, 1 (January 1968): 5–26. This essay and others like it are examples of a reform-oriented approach and are primarily concerned with how well librarians deliver professional services. Only occasionally and very recently has anyone directly challenged the

trait model; see, for example, Leigh Estabrook, "Sociology and Library Research," *Library Trends* 32, 4 (Spring 1984): 472.

5. The philosophical background of this critique of definition can be found in many places. Two of the more famous are Ludwig Wittgenstein, *Philosophical Investigations*, trans. G. E. M. Anscombe (Oxford: Blackwell's, 1953); and W. V. O. Quine, *Word and Object* (Cambridge: MIT Press, 1960).

6. On the distinction between the professions in the two traditions, see Everett Hughes, *The Sociological Eye* (New Brunswick, NJ: Transaction Books, 1984); and Dietrich Rueschemeyer, "Professional Autonomy and the Social Control of Expertise," *Sociology of the Professions: Lawyers, Doctors, and Others*, eds. Robert Dingwall and Philip Lewis (London: Macmillan, 1968).

7. In what follows I rely on a comprehensive critical survey of the sociology of the professions by Paul Dorsey, *Accountability and University Teaching: Toward the Systematic Mediation of Professional Power*, unpublished Ph.D. dissertation, Western Michigan University, 1980.

8. Talcott Parsons, "Professions," *International Encyclopedia of the Social Sciences* (New York: Macmillan, 1968).

9. This summary is taken from a much more comprehensive account in Don Martindale, *The Nature and Types of Sociological Theory* (Boston: Houghton Mifflin, 1981), pp. 445ff.

10. Ibid., pp. 464ff., 501ff.

11. An "institution," in this view, is not a kind of organization—for example, a hospital or a prison—although some sociologists do use the term in that way as most of us do in ordinary affairs.

12. Terence Johnson, *Professions and Power* (London: Macmillan, 1977), pp. 29–30. Two other key figures in this rethinking of the subject are Eliot Freidson and Dietrich Rueschemeyer, whose work has been cited a number of times. A spirited attack on the traditional sociological study of the professions, which is in general agreement with the control approach, is provided by Julius Roth, "Professionalism: The Sociologist's Decoy," *Sociology of Work and Occupations* 1, 1 (February 1974): 6–23. For an example of some of the rethinking of the study of professions among historians, see Gerald L. Geison, ed., *Professions and Professional Ideologies in America* (Chapel Hill: University of North Carolina Press, 1983).

13. The reader who is interested in the philosophical background of this general line of thought can see Gilbert Ryle, "Systematically Misleading Expressions," *Logic and Language, First Series*, ed. Anthony Flew (New York: Oxford University Press, 1951), pp. 11–36; and Gilbert Ryle, *The Concept of Mind* (New York: Barnes and Noble, 1949).

14. Johnson, *Professions and Power*, pp. 29ff.; Douglas Klegon, "The Sociology of the Professions: An Emerging Perspective," *Sociology of Work and Occupations* 5 (August 1978): 259–83.

15. Johnson, *Professions and Power*, pp. 8, 29–30.

16. Richard H. Hall and Gloria V. Engel, "Autonomy and Expertise: Threats and Barriers to Occupational Autonomy," *Varieties of Work Experience*, eds. Phyllis Stewart and Muriel G. Cantor (Canmbridge, MA: Schenkman, 1974), pp. 7–20; and Marie R. Haug and Marvin B. Sussman, "Professional Autonomy and the Revolt of the Client," *Social Problems* 17 (Fall 1969): 153–60.

17. Dorsey, *Accountability and University Teaching*, pp. 6ff.

18. Richard Hall, "The Social Construction of the Professions," *Sociology of Work and Occupations* 6 (February 1979): 124–26.

19. For example, Wilbert Moore, *The Professions: Roles and Rules* (New York: Russell Sage Foundation, 1970), where autonomy is counted as the central functional characteristic; Phyllis Stewart and Murel G. Cantor, "The Social Context of Occupations," *Varieties of Work Experience*, eds. Phyllis Stewart and Murel G. Cantor, pp. 7–20.

20. Eliot Friedson, *The Profession of Medicine: A Study in the Sociology of Applied Knowledge* (New York: Dodd, Mead, 1970); Dorsey, *Accountability and University Teaching*, pp. 10ff.

21. H. H. Jamous and B. Pelloile, "Professions as Self-Perpetuating Systems: Changes in the French University Hospital System," *Professions and Professionalisation*, ed. John A. Jackson (Cambridge: Cambridge University Press, 1970), pp. 111–52.

22. Chapter 2.

23. Johnson, *Professions and Power*, pp. 43, 51–53.

24. Terence Johnson, "The Professions in the Class Structure," *Industrial Society: Class, Cleavage, and Control*, ed. Richard Scase (New York: St. Martin's Press, 1977), pp. 93–110.

25. The corporate invasion of the health-care field is described in detail by Paul Starr, *The Social Transformation of American Medicine* (New York: Basic Books, 1982).

26. A much more fully developed Marxist theory of the professions is presented by Larson, who argues that professionalization is the process of an occupation obtaining and holding market power. This involves the creation of a market for services, a demand for special status in the overall system of occupational prestige, and the legitimation of this status. Magali S. Larson, *The Rise of Professionalism: A Sociological Analysis* (Berkeley: University of California Press, 1977), pp. 47–48, 50. See also Magali S. Larson, "The Production of Expertise and the Constitution of Expert Power," *The Authority of Experts: Studies in History and Theory*, ed. Thomas Haskell, (Bloomington: Indiana University Press, 1984), pp. 28–80.

27. Everett Hughes, *The Sociological Eye* (New Brunswick, NJ: Transaction Books, 1984), p. 372.

28. For example, Nina Toren, "Deprofessionalization and Its Sources: A Preliminary Analysis," *Sociology of Work and Occupations* 2 (November 1975): 323–37; Marie Haug, "Deprofessionalization: An Alternative Hypothesis for the Future," *Professionalization and Social Change*, ed. Paul Halmos (Keele, England: University of Keele Press, 1973), pp. 195–211; and Marie Haug, "The Deprofessionalization of Everyone?" *Sociological Focus* 8 (August, 1975): 197–213.

29. Haug, "Deprofessionalization," pp. 200–201; also Hall and Engel, "Autonomy and Expertise."

30. Ralph M. Edwards, "The Management of Libraries and the Professional Functions of Librarians," *Library Quarterly* 45 (April 1975): 150–60.

31. The key source is Harry Braverman, *Labor and Monopoly Capital* (New York: Monthly Review Press, 1974); but see also Michael Burawoy, *Manufacturing Consent: Changes in the Labor Process Under Monopoly Capitalism* (Chicago: University of Chicago Press, 1979); Dan Clawson, *Bureaucracy and the Labor Process: The Transformation of U.S. Industry, 1860–1920* (New York: Monthly Review Press, 1980).

32. William J. Reeves, *Librarians as Professionals: The Occupation's Impact on Library Work Arrangements* (Lexington, MA: Lexington Books, 1980). This is the only

empirical study of librarianship based mainly on the occupational approach to the study of professions. It is essential reading.

33. See, for example, Ruth Hafter, *Academic Librarians and Cataloging Networks* (Westport, CT: Greenwood, 1985).

34. Brian Nielsen, "Online Bibliographic Searching and the Deprofessionalization of Librarianship," *Online Review* 4 (September 1980): 215–24.

35. Dorsey, "Accountability and University Teaching," pp. 12ff.; Eliot Freidson, "The Changing Nature of Professional Control," *Annual Review of Sociology* 10 (1984): 1–20.

4

The Keepers of the Keys: Librarianship as Occupational Control

POWER, AUTHORITY, AND CONTROL

Power, in its purest form, is the ability to force someone to behave in a certain way. The pure form is evident at numerous points in our daily existence: the child who is picked up and carried to bed, the criminal who is put in prison, the employee who is given a final warning and then fired. But if social life were based only on the purest form of power, it would be hardly more than a form of organized terrorism. And, of course, at times that is just what it is, for in certain situations the broader spectrum of control vanishes. But such situations are inherently unstable, though they may be relatively long-lasting, and the use of naked power is in the long run a very ineffective and dangerous way to exercise control. This can be easily seen from numerous political situations in which powerful forces attempt to subvert subtler forms of control and succeed only in producing disorder, confusion, and despair.

Pure force, then, is always part of the background of social life, but it is normally complemented by much more subtle and effective mechanisms of control. The term *authority* is sometimes used to refer to what makes the exercise of control seem to be legitimate or acceptable. If a certain means for controlling behavior is accepted as proper and is based on some shared sense of what is right, it has authority, or is perceived as legitimate.[1] We use the term *authority* in that way here to call attention to the fact that in most cases what makes people behave in certain predictable ways is not so much that they fear they will be disgraced or humiliated if they do not, but because there is a social consensus on what is right and wrong in certain social situations, and because this sense of right and wrong becomes part of the individual's way of thinking. Thus it is really authority that assures a reasonable level of compliant behavior, through legitimation of power.

As in most social settings, the use of brute force in work is relatively rare. Control in work is supported and legitimated by special forms of authority. Some are rooted in the occupation and thus are expressions of a kind of collective occupational autonomy: they express the group's will. But other forms of authoritative control come from sources external to the occupation. Thus we need to be aware at the outset of the distinction between "occupational" and, for example, "managerial" or "administrative" control. Virtually all professional workers at some point experience limitations on their freedom from these sources. Nonetheless, many functions in complex organizations are carried out and controlled by persons whose authority is derived from the occupational group to which they belong, and not from the local organizational setting or from its managers.

TWO TYPES OF OCCUPATIONAL AUTHORITY

Types of authority vary rather widely throughout the occupational structure; in collegially controlled or professionalized work groups, there are two predominant types: normative and structural.[2] This discussion of the two types of authority takes us into the heart of the occupational control approach to the study of librarianship.

Normative Authority

Normative authority is based on collective agreement, or group cohesion, which refers to the fact that practitioners generally share ways of thinking, problem solving, and types of professional behavior. The overall similarity of thinking and acting gives the group a certain strength to control work routines. Normative authority has three major sources.

First, there is the professional or graduate school charged with the initial stage of the educational process. In the professional school, the knowledge and skill are cultivated and transmitted to new workers, and a distinctive occupational identity begins to form. The cultivation of the knowledge base of the field naturally requires a certain distance from the immediacy of actual work situations. For this reason, library educators generally have more in common with other university teachers than they do with practitioners, and this is always the case in professional education.

The second source of normative authority is a set of professional associations providing general standards for routine work, definitions of professionalism, broad statements of policy affecting the delivery of services, clarifications of the basic attitudes and values underlying the work, and support for research and scholarship to improve professional practice. In librarianship there is a central national association (the American Library Association), which is the key member of the set, and a subgroup of national specialized associations under its control: the Association of College and Research Libraries, Reference and Adult Services Division, Resources and Technical Services Division, and others. In librarianship there are also independent national associations based on occupational specialization: the Special Libraries Association, the Medical Library Association, and others.

The third source is the actual work setting, where professionals develop job descriptions, formulate policies, and determine priorities for implementing them. They decide who is to do materials selection, answer different types of reference questions, and how materials are to be acquired and processed. In many cases they also determine how professionals and other employees are to be evaluated and rewarded, and how money for research and equipment will be spent. Here the knowledge base and the professional identity first encountered in school and the activities of the associations are put to use in the delivery of services to clients and in the management of the library as an organization. What goes on in the work setting is naturally not a simple repetition of what was learned in school or absorbed from official statements from the associations, but these form the background of the cohesion found in the actual setting. Because practitioners share broad areas of agreement from common educational and professional backgrounds, they are able to develop new forms of cohesion in their home organizations. Ideally, the three sources of normative authority work together to reinforce control. The details of how cohesion is established vary significantly from one situation to the next.[3]

Structural Authority

In structural authority, the basis of the occupation's control over its activities is found in the legal power with which the occupation has been vested by legislative bodies and government agencies. This official power is based ultimately on the position of the occupation in the economic market of services. The stronger the market situation for the occupation, the more structural control predominates. In these cases, legally binding sanctions control access to the profession, exercise control over the curricula of the schools, and regulate the conduct of practitioners. In the structural type, in other words, the profession, through its professional associations and other professional agencies, has a recognized legal authority.

It is important to note here that structural authority is found in varying degrees in all occupations and can be extremely strong in certain groups that have never made any claim to professional status. The contract work of plumbers, electricians, construction supervisors, and many related types of "blue-collar" work, for example, is often strictly regulated and protected by elaborate legal mechanisms. There is, in other words, no essential relationship between structural authority and collegially controlled, or professional, work, even if the two are sometimes found together.

The two types are presented here as if they were quite distinct, but occupational authority is usually a mix of the normative and the structural foundations of action, and the actual degree of the mix must be determined by looking closely at individual professions. Certainly in medicine and law there is a very strong structural component, along with an almost equally strong normative one. Professional associations in these fields exercise legal authority over entrance to the occupation and many aspects of professional behavior.

As the market value of a service declines, the predominance of the structural component declines, and the importance of the normative component increases. Reeves, in the study of librarianship already cited, shows that the normative foundation guarantees a high degree of control in librarianship, even though librarianship, like other occupations, does not have a particularly strong market position. Thus even though the demand for library services is weaker than the demand for medical, legal, and some other types of services, the normative aspect of authority assures a considerable degree of control over work. On the basis of his findings, Reeves argues quite convincingly that it is a mistake to assume that structural authority is a unique condition of occupational control.[4] Much of the doubt about the library occupation's claim to professional status is based on the implicit assumption of structural authority. If Reeves is correct, this assumption is not valid, and this doubt should no longer prevail.

The Interaction of Normative and Structural Authority

Reeves depicts interaction of normative and structural foundations in a useful two-by-two table that shows occupational control as a function of authority type mix (Fig. 4–1).[5] The table presents dimensions of strength and weakness for normative and structural foundations. Reading horizontally, normative foundations range from relatively weak ("minimal") to relatively strong ("elaborated"); reading vertically, structural foundations can be strong ("high") or weak ("low").

Looking at the interactive relationships between the two types of authority, the important point is that no occupation is without some market-based structural control, and no occupation is able to function entirely without normatively authorized control either. For most occupations showing collegial control, it is the normative foundation that predominates. On the other hand, even in cases where occupational control is based on the strongest structural foundations, it is still necessary to base most of the actual work on the normative foundations.[6] In other words, what provides the occupation with its routine cohesiveness is a set of shared attitudes, values, concepts, and intellectual orientations toward work. By itself, legally based power cannot do this.

Librarianship generally fits into the category of "variable authority," because most of the occupation's control over work is based on the cohesion that comes from the normative foundations. As in all occupations, there is a structural component of this authority based on the effective demand for librarians' services, but in comparison to some other occupations, the structural component is relatively weak.[7] By the same token, librarianship's market situation is roughly comparable to certain other highly professionalized groups, such as college teaching. For example, construction work would show a strong market position

Figure 4—1
Interaction of Normative and Structural Foundations

NORMATIVE FOUNDATIONS

	Miminal	Elaborated
H I G H	Low authority (e.g. union control)	High authority
STRUCTURAL FOUNDATIONS		
L O W	No authority (management control)	Variable authority

Source: William J. Reeves, *Librarianship as a Profession: The Occupation's Impact on Library Work Arrangements* (Lexington, MA: Lexington Books, 1980), p. 14.

(except of course, during an economic downturn) and thus a relatively strong structural foundation. At the same time it would show a minimally elaborated normative foundation, and thus would not approach the model of collegial control—unionism is the predominant type of control in this occupation. Obviously, the strongest market position and the strongest structural foundation allied with the most elaborated normative foundation provide the most secure type of authority, but it is questionable whether any occupation achieves this in a pure form. At the present time, medicine and law show the strongest forms of both types, and thus enjoy the most secure kind of combined authority and control. Nonetheless, the rapid proliferation of physicians and attorneys in recent years, along with a number of other trends, indicates that this situation is changing and will continue to do so for some considerable time. And very likely, as structural authority decreases in these groups, we can expect to see even greater emphasis placed on normative authority.

MEASURING CONTROL: SOME EVIDENCE

The earlier sections sketch in some of the conceptual background of the occupational control model in librarianship. Even without empirical evidence to lean on, the claims of the occupational control model are strong. Thus we are fortunate in having a thorough empirical study of library work arrangements to provide the evidence to complement developments in the theory of the professions that have gradually qualified the trait and functionalist approaches. When we look carefully at this evidence, it is very difficult not to conclude that the whole professionalization issue needs to be reinterpreted in light of the more recent approach.

As noted, William J. Reeves reported on a 1974 survey to determine the degree of match between general definitions and standards of work—as developed by library associations and library schools—and actual work arrangements in a number of different settings. To do this, it was first necessary to survey the extent to which librarians and other workers in libraries are aware of such definitions and standards. The general conclusion is that a general awareness of the importance of schools and associations, coupled with a commitment to rely on these sources in defining work arrangements, is correlated with high levels of control.[8]

In measuring orientations toward library associations, interest in the profession, the extent to which interests and values were seen as exemplified in work settings, consensus on role expectations, reliance on formal job descriptions, and other variables, Reeves found some variation, particularly for awareness of associations. This variation is attributed generally to differences in work setting or type of library, although it is clear that type of professional specialization plays an important role also.[9] This means that occupational control varies from one library to the next and from one type of library to the next, mainly because the strength of occupational cohesion itself varies from one situation to the next.

Control is most secure in larger organizations with larger acquisitions budgets, particularly, though not exclusively, where the library is an independent agency not situated in a larger organization. On the other hand, control appears somewhat less secure where the library depends on a surrounding nonlibrary organization for its operating support.

A block to control from a rather different source appears in libraries where staff members depend heavily on the expertise of users. Here professional specialty, rather than library type, is the key variable.[10] In this case, a mastery of the knowledge base of librarianship is one kind of control-establishing response, but it is clear that in many instances there will be no substitute for subject competence on the part of the librarian. In some cases, however, where librarians cannot hope to match the subject expertise of the user, the turn toward one's own occupational knowledge base as a form of applied metascience, with its various "keys" to unlocking the mysteries of recorded information, tends to reestablish control that is lost, as the librarian enters a territory closed to the mere subject specialist.

In those cases where occupational orientations show significant awareness of and agreement with the viewpoints of the associations and the schools, there is a strong correlation between general occupational standards and the actual work arrangements of specific settings. In these cases, in other words, the work routines "come up to standard." The strength of the occupational orientations also predicts, as Reeves points out, the degree of role consensus in the organizations, or the extent to which workers of all types agree on job descriptions and work assignments. Not surprisingly, the very existence of formal job descriptions is by itself a predictor of strong occupational orientations, and thus usually is found only in settings where librarians control the work routines.

Applying this to the types of library organizations familiar to the practitioner, the public library, at least where the organization or the system is relatively large and is not directly administered by some outside agency, is an example of the most secure level of control. This comes from its status as an independent library agency, and also, of course, from the tradition of funding the public library directly from tax revenues. In a more general cultural sense, however, it is clear that the position of the public library is partly a reflection of one of the major ideals of democratic government, and, of course, not all library work settings share this advantage.

At the other extreme are certain types of special libraries, particularly in business and government, where control rests with administrators, managers, civil servants, or elected officials. (All the same, it is obvious that not all special libraries fall into this category; some, for example, are directly attached to public or large academic research libraries or, somewhat more rarely, enjoy a position of almost complete independence.) In academic libraries the picture is complicated by certain facts: there are several rather distinctly different subtypes (college, university, major research institution, and so on), sources of funding are external, the library is usually situated in a larger administrative network, and many librarians deal with highly expert users. In the latter case the tendency of many academic libraries to use existing staff in certain areas of collection development, bibliography, and reference work without regard to subject expertise no doubt contributes to loss of control. But in another respect the picture of the academic library is much harder to pin down; this is because it can be extremely complex as an organization and can house so many different kinds of occupational subtypes, including many different types of librarians.

The other major familiar type of library is the school library or the school media center. School libraries are rather different organizationally from any of the other major types; so different, in fact, that they are in a sense out of the picture altogether. In terms of the themes explored here, the distinguishing characteristic of the school library is what Pauline Wilson has called "encapsulation" within a completely different occupational group.[11] This means that the library occupation does not really control the work of school librarians, since they follow standards derived from teacher certification programs, and from major professional associations in primary and secondary education. At first meeting, this fact of encapsulation suggests that school librarians and libraries show a relatively low degree of control. But one might argue just as cogently that encapsulation indicates something much more radical: perhaps school libraries, from an organizational point of view, are simply a subtype of educational organization and should not be compared to other types of libraries at all.

LIBRARIANSHIP AS A COLLEGIALLY CONTROLLED OCCUPATION

We can now relate some of the findings from the Reeves study to the theory of occupational control introduced in Chapter 3. We saw there the emergence of a three-part model in the sociological critiques of the trait theory and functionalism.[12] We also suspect, from attempts at applying some of these findings to librarianship, that the occupation is relatively heterogeneous, for it contains a number of distinct subtypes or specialties, and also a number of distinct occupational settings: public, special, academic, school, and others. In relating the empirical findings on work arrangements to developments in the theory of the professions, we need to keep in mind that this heterogeneity by itself complicates the picture considerably and causes problems in making blanket statements about the occupation as a whole.

This aside, Reeves's study suggests that librarianship shows a high degree of collegial control. It is also clear that in some cases the types of control in librarianship are mixed with a certain amount of mediation and client control, just as they often are in other middle-class occupations. We saw that public librarians appear, at least in the areas of reference and selection, to most closely fit the collegial model. But even here there will be some mediation from some of the sources identified earlier: external managerial control, public attempts to influence library policies, the expertise of professionals in other fields (particularly in automation), and others. Academic libraries show pockets of mediation and significant amounts of collegial control, and special libraries are closer than any other type to client control, although no setting is purely controlled by users. The situation of the school librarian, as noted, is so unusual that it is difficult to use the occupational control model for interpretation. Like all librarians, school librarians work in situations where there is a significant amount of mediation, but this observation can be made only by comparing school librarians directly with other types of librarians and ignoring their crucial relation to education. Thus "encapsulation" makes judgments about school librarians very difficult to distinguish from statements about the teaching profession.

The findings of the empirical study of work arrangements include variations in the degree of control as a function of change in occupational setting or type of library. Working in a different direction, we can use Reeves's study in another way, as some evidence for the claim of heterogeneity itself. That librarianship, in other words, is a relatively fragmented or "balkanized" occupation is something that practitioners know through experience. Here the empirical findings shed some light on how that translates into different types of control over work routines. They permit us to say something more specific about how professional work in libraries gets done and who is likely to control it in various settings. But the very heterogeneity of the occupation seems to exert a counteracting force toward unity, and in fact we find a consistent reliance throughout the profession (with the possible exception of school librarianship as noted) on central associations and professional education programs. This suggests the great importance of the associations and the schools in supplying and then reinforcing some of the group cohesion that is lost in the development of subspecialties and types of work setting. Clearly the occupation has become much more specialized in recent years and will no doubt continue in this direction. And this in turn suggests that the associations and the schools will have, if anything, an even greater responsibility to provide a shared sense of professional identity.

Reference Work as Collegial Control

To illustrate collegial control more specifically, let us look at reference work, partly because it is a central professional function but also because it is heavy on direct contact with clients. Face-to-face interaction with the user of the service is, of course, not unique to collegially or professionally controlled work situations, nor is it necessary to them. But when situated within a collegially controlled work situation, direct client contact does have a certain importance for professionals, for it is an important place to demonstrate control over the delivery of services.

Traditionally, interaction is initiated by the client and terminated by the professional. A patient goes to a doctor to describe symptoms; a client approaches a lawyer to take a case; a user goes to a reference librarian with certain expressed information needs. In each case, the professional translates the expressed need into an effective need; and in many of these cases, the user will know that there is a problem to be solved, but not precisely what the problem is, or how to express it, or indeed even the most basic vocabulary required to express it. Obviously this places considerable emphasis on the skill of the professional in understanding and defining user need, and it requires a special "human relations" or communicative ability that is not directly related to the substantive knowledge that the professional uses in delivering the services.

One particularly good example of the translation process occurs in online searching, where there is a complex interplay between the specialized vocabulary of the user, the technical vocabulary needed to search the data base, and the ordinary language vocabulary used by both parties as the assumed background of the whole process. Ordinary language sentences are used as the setting for both user-specific and searcher-specific vocabularies, and it is the searcher who must be able to see that the user's vocabulary may or may not be of use in performing the search. It is also the searcher who must be able to explain that the process of translating user jargon into acceptable indexing language does not eliminate essential shades of meaning. The implied knowledge of data base systems and indexing languages is only a minimal condition of being able to deliver the service, for the broader skills of communication and negotiation are equally essential. This example of online searching should not obscure the fact that this is basically true of all reference work. What may not be quite so evident is that these communicative skills—particularly the laborious processes of translation—are also essential when professionals deal with each other, and so they apply to a greater or lesser degree even for professional workers who have little or no contact with clients.

The Reeves study shows that reference work exhibits a high degree of collegial control, and he cites as evidence the substantial overlap between standards developed in schools and associations and work arrangements. His evidence also shows a high degree of consensus on role expectations for performing the basic functions of reference and selection.[13] Librarians and other library workers, in other words, look to official occupational statements to define reference work and also to occupational norms to define different types of reference service and to determine who will provide it. An additional reason may be that the very nature of the professional-client relationship calls for collegial control, and thus it is highly appropriate to look to reference work as an important indicator of collegial control in librarianship. Aside from the Reeves study, there are not a great many investigations to use as data sources for further interpretation, but there is the work already cited on online searching as a subspecialty of reference. The more the reference librarian is distinguished as a specialist in certain types of work or in certain subject areas, the more remote he or she is from the provision of general information, which falls increasingly to the paraprofessional or clerical worker. And the technical aspects of machine searching only add to the librarian's control over the interaction with the user.[14]

Selection as Collegial Control

Selection, like reference, is part of the Reeves study because it is one of the central professional tasks. Deciding what does or does not go into the collection assumes a great deal: knowledge of the fields covered, of user needs, of the current state of the collection, and a number of other things that make selection unlikely to come under client control in any direct way. But there are mediating factors that qualify or otherwise influence control. One is the reliance on various kinds of acquisitions profiles, which include approval plans, standing orders, blanket orders, and related devices. In these cases the acquisitions process in effect assumes priority over selection, but this does not really cause a major block to collegial control. Interestingly, it is a mediating factor that really enhances control.

There are two reasons for this. The first is that acquisitions specialists are librarians, and thus control is merely passing from one professional to another. The passage of control from one specialist to another may be a very important issue for the persons involved, but it does not mean a loss of control in collegial terms: professional control is a corporate, not a personal phenomenon. The second and more important reason is that profile selection does not really replace the more difficult and interesting selection decisions, but only the more routine and obvious ones. Thus it frees the selector to do the much more complicated work of selecting material that is harder to track or requires specialized knowledge. This might be subject expertise, but it could also be knowledge of trends in publishing or a familiarity with the problems of dealing with certain formats. Any selector will automatically choose items from major publishers in certain subject fields, and thus this kind of selection is highly amenable to profile ordering anyway. But deciding to do retrospective buying of out-of-print titles—perhaps even to design unusual or specialized buying programs in this area—or to buy materials in foreign languages, or whether or not to buy machine-readable data files or microform sets of archival materials are examples of selection activities that cannot easily be made routine.

Perhaps even more important, profile ordering frees the selector to evaluate and assess collections by subject area, and thus to be in a position to see problem areas that need special attention. In the same vein, it also frees selectors to become more knowledgeable in a general way about the bibliographic organization of the fields they cover, and about the populations they serve. They can undertake studies of literature use and patterns of communication to supplement their current level of knowledge. Thus if we say that profile ordering in some way affects the role of the selector, we would have to conclude that it has enhanced rather than inhibited collegial control.

We have noted the expertise of the user as another factor. In both reference and selection, particularly in special libraries, there is a fair amount of mediation from user expertise. And, of course, a complete reliance on user expertise for selection decisions very much inhibits collegial control. Despite the mediation, selection has on the whole become far too complex for most library users to understand, let alone to carry out on their own. As the older fields of knowledge develop, and as new fields appear, there emerge new types of library users, some with very advanced levels of subject knowledge. At the same time, however, there is a parallel development in the complexity of the overall bibliographic organization that is required to control these developments, and a corresponding requirement for specialized understanding of that organization and how to exploit it. And the expertise of the most advanced user normally does not include this kind of knowledge. Thus users increasingly find that the problems of bibliographic organization found in selection are best left to librarians. Accordingly, as selection passes from outside experts to librarians whose qualifications and experience include both the forms and the contents of bodies of literature, selection approaches the collegial model. Since this has been occurring in the academic library since the 1940s, it can be taken as a very well established trend.[15]

SPECIALIZATION AND CONTROL

We have discussed in a general way how certain key functions in librarianship relate to collegial control in professional work, and in doing so we concentrated on reference, selection, and subject specialization. It seems clear, however, that specialization by itself has a significant effect on control. It is true, in other words, that the functions so far discussed have a particularly close relationship to the collegial style, for reasons already indicated. At the same time the general tendency for work roles to become increasingly specialized by itself has control-enhancing features. This is probably true in all occupations, where the trend toward specialization makes it difficult for the nonspecialist to acquire the knowledge necessary to control the work routine except in the most general managerial sense. Supervisors or managers may control certain important conditions of employment, such as personnel review processes or career ladders, but they cannot effectively control the actual process of delivering the service unless they have the specialized knowledge that this requires. Specialization thus creates a certain zone of freedom within which the worker operates. In occupations dominated entirely by managerial control, this freedom is extremely limited and does not by itself guarantee a significant amount of autonomy. Where specialization is combined with collegial traditions, however, it seems only to enhance the amount of professional control.

Thus the importance of reference, selection, and subject specialization should not obscure the fact of a general trend. The academic library—particularly but not exclusively in the major academic research institution—is now composed of many different types of specialties. A study for the Council on Library Resources, for example, distinguishes at least five types: functional (reference, bibliography, circulation, technical services), user group (undergraduate, graduate and faculty, returning adult), format or special material type (maps, microforms, machine-readable files, government publications), subject, and departmental or branch specializations.[16] And this is true of other library types as well, as anyone familiar with a large public library system can easily confirm. In fact, it is even true of a considerable number of college libraries, which is not surprising, since the socioeconomic trends that have led to specialization in the major research institutions are also having a similar effect on the production and dissemination of information sources for the general population. And where this is true, specialization may be expected to produce results paralleling those already outlined for reference, selection, and computer searching—enhancing collegial control.

Mediation or Deprofessionalization?

In looking at the results of this interpretation of Reeves's findings, we see a mix of control types. In Chapter 3 we considered the three-part division of collegial, mediated, and client control, and suggested that collegially controlled work groups had indeed suffered some "mediation" from outside forces. At the same time, collegially controlled groups do not appear to have reverted to complete control by clients. Does the existence of "mediated" or mixed control spell deprofessionalization? The most we can say for sure is that if we hold certain very traditional views about the professions—for example, the kinds of views described in discussing the trait theory and the functionalist theory—we must conclude that all occupations have been deprofessionalized. But that tells us nothing in particular about librarianship, and it may be only another way of saying that it fits a general pattern of evolution in the occupational structure. Obviously, if we choose our examples properly, we can find instances of tasks performed by professionals that have been altered so significantly that they can no longer properly be considered part of professional work. (This is probably most notable in technical services, where automation has made its most visible impact.)

But while this might enable us to conclude, for certain types of jobs or certain types of libraries, that there are deprofessionalizing forces, it is just as clear that in many other areas of librarianship what is really happening is the emergence of new forms of occupational control. And some of these, as we have seen, are much closer to the collegial control model than they are to either client control or advanced degrees of mediation. Our conclusions depend on our theoretical commitments and on how we use them to interpret findings from the literatures of sociology and librarianship. If we find the occupational control model of professionalization to be persuasive, we will conclude that "deprofessionalization" is occurring only in some areas, while in others professionalization continues because greater control is being exercised. What we should not conclude is that any suspicion of divergence from the older definitions of professionalism automatically indicates a total loss of professional status, or shows conclusive evidence of deprofessionalization. For what such a divergence shows, among other things, is the failure of the older theories to grasp the nature of contemporary professional work.

KNOWLEDGE, AUTONOMY, AND CONTROL

Reeves's findings are also useful in interpreting in a general way the role of autonomy in library work, and thus touch upon one of the central dimensions of professionalization. In particular they support the claim that a strong orientation toward the occupation affects both of Freidson's "zones of autonomy."[17] Collectively held work standards derived from the associations and the schools cover, in other words, both the special zone, which includes routine skill and task definitions, and the general zone, which contains basic values and goals of the occupation as a whole.[18]

The occupational control approach has particularly important implications for the large question of the relation between the knowledge base, autonomy, and control over work routines. We saw earlier that in order to support autonomy, the knowledge base must have enough indeterminacy to elude control from outside forces.[19] Its leading ideas, its integrating principles, and its underlying values must, in other words, be relatively abstract and relatively complex. Yet the knowledge base must not be too indeterminate, or it loses its relation to technical concerns and becomes indistinguishable from the traditional fields of liberal learning. The knowledge base must strike a difficult balance between techniques and skills on the one hand and abstract ideas on the other. To assure this, technique must bear within itself a theoretical complexity and must be related to leading ideas. Practice must be difficult to master, must require some use of judgment and imagination, and must provide opportunities for generating new ideas. Conversely, the ideas themselves must be practice-oriented.

In a collegially controlled occupation, technicality and indeterminacy must be interwoven, each rooted in the other. This supports autonomy for the occupation as a whole, because it protects practice from encroachment and outside control, and general principles from irrelevance. The proper relationship between the technical and the abstract successfully unites Freidson's special and general zones of autonomy. If the ideas are specific enough to be useful in transforming technique, and if the techniques have the intellectual complexity that requires sustained ability and attention, the special zone of routine tasks becomes closely connected to the general zone of ideas and values. There remains, of course, a verbal or analytical distinction between the two, but the precise boundary between them is not at all easy to specify.

The practical question this raises is whether the knowledge base of the occupation makes a direct contribution to maintaining occupational cohesion, and thus reinforces occupational control over work routines. It seems clear on intuitive grounds that it does do this, but understanding the process is a very complex matter. How does a body of knowledge come to play a part in the formation of a shared identity, and thus enhance practitioners' ability to control their work routines? We are in effect asking how a body of knowledge becomes part of a shared style of working. Just as there is a certain style of work in medicine or law that reflects the state of medical and legal knowledge, there will be something similar in librarianship, corresponding to the way in which the knowledge base gets translated into shared ways of accomplishing routines.

The link between the knowledge base as cultivated in the professional school and the work setting is the character or identity of the group as a whole. If this identity is formed in a certain way in the school and this formation is reinforced by association policies, then the knowledge base has a direct line of transmission into practical settings. Taken by itself, knowledge does not necessarily find its way into practice, but if it has been internalized by practitioners and if its interests are adequately represented by the policy-making activities of relevant associations, it acquires some of its own power in generating agreement and creating solidarity in the group. When this occurs the practical activities of the group bring professional knowledge to life in a work setting. Theory becomes practice, and practice becomes theoretically informed.

THE TWO CULTURES OF PROFESSIONALISM: THE COGNITIVE AND THE NORMATIVE

A body of knowledge is composed of general intellectual orientations, concepts, propositions, skills, and techniques used in accomplishing ordinary routines. It ranges all the way from loosely held views of the world in general to extremely specialized concepts that make sense only in the most restricted contexts of professional service. Librarianship is generally oriented toward the intellectual tasks of organization for access. Its conceptual apparatus is thus expressed typically in propositions, generalizations, or other statements that share this general orientation.

Classification schemes, for example, respect certain basic principles: classes must be hospitable to expansion or contraction; their members must be arranged in a manner consistent with specified logical relationships; and their notational schemes must respect the same principles. Something similar is true for controlled vocabularies, as even the most inexperienced librarian knows from using the Library of Congress Subject Headings, the ERIC Thesaurus, or the descriptor lists of many periodical indexes.[20] Bodies of literature reflect certain generalizations applicable to the behavior of persons engaged in accumulating, disseminating, and applying the results of inquiry: patterns of communication vary, are more or less informal, authors cite a greater or lesser number of other authors in writing up their results. And, of course, the same is true for user populations, since the consumption of the results of inquiry is subject to many of the same discernible regularities. Users rely more or less heavily on review publications in certain fields but not in others; they place greater or lesser emphasis on patterns of citation of previous literature; they use or do not use certain tools for access and review.

At the delivery of service level, the conceptual framework underlies the application of the specific skills and techniques used in cataloging, reference, selection, acquisitions, and such. This approach to knowledge suggests something that is, relatively speaking, value-neutral: the ideas, general principles, skills, and techniques can in principle be used by anyone and carry no specific reference to ethical or cultural values. But this is an artificial, if useful distinction, for every body of knowledge has not only a cognitive, or "instrumental," dimension, which has to do with how people use a shared set of ideas as tools designed to accomplish certain tasks, but also a normative or value-laden dimension.[21] And while we certainly can draw an analytical distinction between the dimensions, in practice the two are intimately blended. The normative dimension, one might say, reflects the ideology of the group, for it expresses fundamental values.

In Chapter 1 we described the knowledge base of librarianship as a form of applied metascience concerned with three forms of cognitive organization:

- The organization of knowledge (as reflected, for example, in different schemes of knowledge classification and subsequently translated into schemes of document classification).
- The organization of bibliographic information as reflected in the theory and practice of indexing.
- The informal organization of bodies of literature.

These three elements represent the cognitive-instrumental dimension of the knowledge base, and thus as a description are incomplete, for the intellectual capital of the field includes the normative-ideological dimension as well. In librarianship this dimension is provided by the theory of intellectual freedom, more specifically by the value attached to freedom of access to information. Without the ideology of free access, the cognitive-instrumental component is reduced to the manipulation of a static body of "knowledge" defined by received authority and not by free inquiry. On the other hand, without the cognitive component, the value system loses its relevance to the field. In this way librarianship reproduces within itself the two cultures of science and humane learning.[22] Put in a slightly different way, the cognitive dimension provides us with our most direct access, while the normative component provides some assurance that we are gaining access to something of value to us.

Although we cannot detail here the justification for the cognitive-instrumental and the normative-ideological continuum, we can point out that in outline it would be very similar to the defense of a similar continuum between scientific method and the values of freedom of inquiry. Even though scientific work generally proceeds without much awareness of this continuum, it would nonetheless be impossible without a rigorous ideology of intellectual freedom to support its orientation toward providing empirical evidence to support hypotheses. The value-neutrality often claimed for science ultimately depends on the values expressed in the normative dimension: freedom of access to information, freedom to work creatively, and so on. Since none of these values can be defended by appeal to empirical evidence, their justification must be pragmatic, which, of course, links science with the world of commonsense reasoning from which it seeks to distinguish itself. Scientific method, in other words, rests on our belief that it is good or important to discover the truth about the world, and that this discovery may in some way prove of benefit to us. Similarly, the cognitive-instrumental world of information retrieval, with its schemes and rules of cataloging and classification, its principles of bibliometrics and its empirical generalizations about user behavior, cannot do its job without the underlying belief in the value of freedom of access.

The two dimensions of the knowledge base have a special relevance to the maintenance of autonomy and control in work settings. It seems clear that the more purely cognitive side of professional knowledge is most closely related to the "special zone" of autonomy, to the zone of routine tasks. What is less clear at this point, and more difficult to clarify, is how the knowledge base is related to the general zone, the zone of basic assumptions about service and the realization of certain human values that are intimately connected with its delivery. It is the normative dimension that provides this connection. For this reason, when we discuss the knowledge base in relation to autonomy and control, we need to include the value dimension as well as the scientific. And, of course, the normative dimension must show the same range of complexity, the same tendency to vary along the axis of technicality and indeterminacy. The normative dimension must, in other words, exhibit a similar position on the axis of the technical and the abstract: it must be abstract enough to avoid mere routine, technical enough to avoid empty generality. Certainly the theory of intellectual freedom fits in this category, for it presents so many problems of a theoretical and practical nature, particularly in the area of the First Amendment, that it offers lifetimes of work.[23] Since this is also true of the cognitive dimension of the knowledge base, we may conclude that the knowledge base as a whole has a significant effect on both zones of autonomy.

NOTES

1. The idea of authority as legitimate power or control is widespread; in recent times it is closely associated with Max Weber. For background, see Robert L. Peabody, "Authority," *International Encyclopedia of the Social Sciences* (New York: Macmillan, 1968).

2. William J. Reeves, *Librarians as Professionals: The Occupation's Impact on Library Work Arrangements* (Lexington, MA: Lexington Books, 1980), pp. 11–12, 33–34, 97.

3. For details on a variety of such situations see Reeves, *Librarians as Professionals*, pp. 37ff.

4. Ibid., pp. 12–13ff.

5. Ibid., p. 14.

6. Ibid., pp. xix–xx, 13.

7. As a whole, "information workers" are in a relatively good position, making up nearly 45 percent of the current labor force, but librarians make up less than 10 percent of these approximately 1.64 million workers. The weakness of the market situation is probably a compound of relatively low demand and small numbers in comparison to the rest of the information industry. This is certainly suggested at any rate by the most comprehensive study of the industry to date, which analyses the information sector of the United States economy by function and work field. For these and other details, see Anthony Debons et al., *The Information Professional: Survey of an Emerging Field* (New York: Marcel Dekker, 1981), pp. 2–4, 17ff., 54.

8. Reeves, pp. 13–15

9. Ibid., pp. 41ff.

10. Ibid, pp. 101, 103.

11. Pauline Wilson, *Stereotype and Status: Librarians in the United States* (Westport, CT: Greenwood Press, 1982), pp. 172ff.

12. See Chapter 3.

13. Reeves, pp. 25–27, 51.

14. Brian Nielsen, "Online Bibliographic Searching and the Deprofessionalization of Librarianship," *Online Review* 4 (September 1980): 215–24. See also Brian Nielsen, "Technological Change and Professional Identity," *Proceedings: New Information Technologies-New Opportunities* (Champaign: Graduate School of Library and Information Science, University of Illinois, 1982), pp. 101–113.

15. Clarence Leuba, "The Roles of Librarians and Professors," *Drexel Library Quarterly* 4 (April 1968): 110–17; Robert Downs, "The Role of the Academic Librarian, 1876–1976," *College and Research Libraries* 37 (November 1976): 491–502; Frederick M. Messick, "Subject Specialists in Smaller Academic Libraries," *Library Resources and Technical Services* 21 (Fall 1977): 368–74; and J. P. Danton, "The Subject Specialist in National and University Libraries," *Libri* 17 (1967): 49ff.

16. Eldred Smith, *The Specialist Librarian in the Academic Research Library: Report to the Council on Library Resources* (Washington, DC: Council on Library Resources, 1971).

17. This is discussed in Chapter 3. For the background, see Eliot Freidson, *The Profession of Medicine: A Study in the Sociology of Applied Knowledge* (New York: Dodd, Mead, 1970).

18. Reeves's study also suggests one factor that may threaten autonomy and that is unionization, which shifts occupational orientations away from associations and schools and supplies a different ideological emphasis in the arbitration of work disputes. Also, unions tend to recruit heavily from the ranks of nonprofessional workers and thus encourage alliances with other occupations, which in turn attenuates the strength of shared orientations among professional workers (Reeves, pp. 43–44). The claim here is not that unionization has universally negative effects, since this would obviously be untrue, but only that it weakens the occupational cohesion underlying collegial control. Unionization has also been examined from the standpoint of its effect on income, occupational status, and other factors not considered here. See Pauline Wilson, *Stereotype and Status*, pp. 184ff.

19. The background of this distinction between the purely narrow (or the technical) and the purely indeterminate is from H. Jamous and B. Peloille, "Professions as Self-

Perpetuating Systems: Changes in the French University Hospital System," *Professions and Professionalisation*, ed. John A. Jackson (Cambridge: Cambridge University Press, 1970), pp. 111–52.

20. The literature of classification theory and practice is very large. The following represent only a few relevant examples: Fran Hopkins, "General Classification: A Review of Classification Research Group Work," *Library Resources and Technical Services* 17 (Spring 1973): 201–10; Arthur Maltby, "Classification: Logic, Limits, and Levels," *Classification in the 1970's*, ed. Arthur Maltby (London: Clive Bingley, 1976), pp. 9–25; Jack Mills, *A Modern Outline of Library Classification* (London: Chapman and Hall, 1960); A Neelameghan, "Classification Theory," *Encyclopedia of Library and Information Science* (New York: Marcel Dekker, 1971); S. R. Ranganathan, *Prologemena to Library Classification*, 3rd ed. (Bombay: Asia House, 1972). For a bibliographic overview, see Phyllis Richmond, "Reading List in Classification Theory," *Library Resources and Technical Services* 16 (Summer 1972): 364–82.

21. In an earlier context we borrowed Reeves's contrast between "normative" and "structural" types of control; see Chapter 3. Here we use "normative" in a more explicitly ethical sense. It is clear that the two usages are closely related despite the difference of emphasis since both refer to shared standards. Norms, in other words, regulate not only the routine tasks, but also regulate conduct on the ethical level.

22. C. P. Snow, *The Two Cultures: And a Second Look* (Cambridge: Cambridge University Press, 1963). This reading of the normative dimension as "liberal" rests on a contemporary understanding of liberalism. Nonetheless, the meaning of liberalism has changed substantially over the years. The contemporary ideology of librarianship allows great latitude for individual freedom, both for professionals and for library users. But this was not always so, and the ethical commitments of the late nineteenth century and the early twentieth seem authoritarian by comparison. See, for example, Jonathan Lindsey and Ann E. Prentice, *Professional Ethics and Librarians* (Phoenix, AZ: Oryz Press, 1985), for an indication of how paternalistic librarianship's professional ethics once were.

23. David Berninghausen, in *The Flight from Reason* (Chicago: American Library Association, 1975), shows how extremely difficult are some of the problems librarians have faced in defending freedom of access. For an overview of the extraordinary conceptual and legal complexity of the theory of intellectual freedom as a problem in constitutional law, see Thomas I. Emerson, *The System of Freedom of Expression* (New York: Vintage Books, 1970).

5

The Social Context of Control: The Social Background, the Schools, and the Association

Chapter 4 deals with the controlling relation between schools, associations, and work arrangements. In this chapter we expand our viewpoint to clarify some of the larger social context that serves as the background of control and ultimately reinforces it. If the viewpoint of Chapter 4 is analogous to a close-up, this is a wide-angle shot. If occupational institutions like the professional school and the professional association have a strong impact on work arrangements, this is partly because they play such a significant role in the transmission of knowledge, the formation of professional identity, and the setting of standards. But it is also because such institutions are situated in a broader social and cultural world that delegates these tasks to them. And the very fact that the occupation is charged with these tasks is a reflection not only of its social importance but an indication of its power. Occupations become gatekeepers of certain provinces of specialized knowledge and expertise.

In filling in this broader picture, we focus on factors that have a special relevance to the issue of controlling work in librarianship. The first is the general social function of libraries, the maintenance of culture through maintenance of access to knowledge records. In a general sense, it is the importance of this function that legitimates the authority of librarianship as an occupation. The second factor is the importance of liberal education as the educational background of professional work in libraries. The third factor is what we call here the ''culture of inquiry,'' which, through its position in higher education, plays an essential role in defining styles of work in professional occupations. Because librarianship has a special relationship to the world of knowledge and inquiry, it has a special relationship to this culture of inquiry.

The three factors condition the more specialized work of the schools and the associations, and thus indirectly condition the types of control found in the occupation. Ultimately the knowledge transmission and identity forming activities of the school and the standard setting of the association are based on the social function of maintaining continuity of culture; here the school and the

Figure 5–1
Background Factors, Occupational Institutions, and Work Arrangements

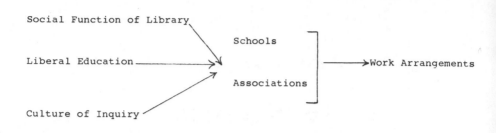

association are affected about equally. The fact that liberal education is the intellectual background of professional work obviously more strongly affects the schools than the associations, but since the major association accredits the professional education programs, it also is affected. In varying degrees the norms of a culture of inquiry are present both in professional education and also in the activities of the association, although perhaps the effect here is most directly on the professional school.

The relations between the social background factors, the occupational institutions, and work arrangements are diagrammed in Figure 5–1.

THE SOCIAL BACKGROUND

The Social Functions of the Library

It is fashionable to raise the question of the ultimate future of libraries and librarians. In certain circles an apocalyptic gloom prevails: librarians appear as an endangered species, and libraries as institutions on the verge of obsolescence. We think of the passenger pigeon, the silent movie, and the debtors' prison.[1] These scenarios make interesting reading, for it is always haunting to meditate one's own demise.

Let us admit, then, that libraries might disappear, and with them librarians and perhaps also paper and hard copy records of knowledge along with it. We might observe, however, that these predictions are almost always made by librarians who work in libraries, and almost invariably on paper, and that others read them on paper, and perhaps reply to them on paper. What is noteworthy is not the prediction—which might or might not come true—but the overwhelming counterweight of the historical tradition. Even if libraries disappeared tomorrow, they would at that point have existed for many thousands of years, and for that reason alone would exert a great influence on social and cultural life for centuries afterward. Professional librarianship, although perhaps not quite as old as the institutions, is even by conservative estimates at least three centuries old; and both libraries and librarians continue to thrive and appear in roughly the same modest numbers. So for the present, the foreseeable future, and for an immense stretch of the past, libraries appear to be very durable institutions. And thus even if libraries are disappearing, we need to continue to study them in their historical richness, and to do the same with the occupational group.

It is not accidental that the historical dimension tends to get suppressed in the disappearing library scenario. The reason is that when we ignore historical and cultural continuity, as technologically minded writers often do, we miss one of the basic social functions that libraries and librarians carry out: providing a certain kind of cultural continuity by maintaining access to knowledge records. By leaving out history we are not only ignoring the actual record of libraries and librarianship, we are actually eliminating part of the occupation's reason for being. Thus we could also say that the law and lawyers will disappear if our concern with mediating legal disputes disappears, or that medicine or nursing will disappear when maintaining people's health is no longer of concern. But because maintaining cultural continuity is not something we will easily dispense with, any more than we would easily dispense with justice or health, it is very unlikely that libraries will disappear any time soon. And even if in certain senses they did indeed disappear, the function of maintaining access would almost certainly remain.

Closely related to the disappearing library scenario is the claim, sometimes only implicit, that the fatal flaw in the institution is that it is overly centered on the past and thus misses what is going to happen in the future. Perhaps this accusation is partly true. What concerns us here, however, is not its accuracy, but what it assumes about knowledge and about history. It assumes that knowledge about the past is not particularly important, and by extension an institution that faces too much toward the past is thus not particularly important. This is like arguing that memory is not an important intellectual function because it deals with the past. The point here, once again, is not to discredit the prophets, for we should listen to them, but that this whole line of thinking misses the critical importance of historical knowledge in self-understanding. The working assumption of this discussion is that without the historical dimension of knowledge only the most one-sided and distorted image of the human world can be produced. And thus if libraries and librarians in some sense are oriented toward the historical dimension of knowledge, and if they spend significant amounts of time preserving a cultural and historical record, this is a powerful argument for their importance, even if it does not guarantee their survival.

Thus it is reasonable, and not making a virtue of necessity, to expect that one of the major social and cultural functions of the library is precisely to assist in the provision of long-term continuity in human culture. Libraries, as the German philosopher Schopenhauer argued over a century and a half ago, are part of the social memory, a means for retaining accumulated knowledge in a usable form.[2] This metaphorical comparison of the institution to a mental function appropriately reflects Schopenhauer's commitment to Plato's theory of knowledge. In the Platonic tradition knowledge is a reminiscence or a recalling of something, and the things that are known must be kept somewhere before they can be remembered. The librarian assists in the process of recall and thus provides, by mediating between user and the recorded form of the knowledge, a much more general link between social life and the culture on which it is founded. Librarianship, in these terms, is part of the production and reproduction of human culture.

We need not be Platonists to appreciate the aptness of Schopenhauer's comparison. And although nineteenth-century German philosophy was strongly influenced by Greek philosophy, it also came under the sway of a much more recent intellectual current, and the metaphor also reflects this. In this case, it is a powerfully materialistic current, the theory of evolution, which was quickly applied to areas of thought outside biology and became part of the intellectual vernacular of the day. Schopenhauer's metaphor captures both the idealistic and the materialistic roots of mind, for implicit in the image of the library as collective memory is an intriguing evolutionary conception of knowledge and the forms in which it is recorded. It is common to think of libraries as luxuries, places that people in ruder times and places did without and without which they managed to survive. The basis for the view is no doubt the well-founded notion that the systematic production of knowledge requires a certain level of social complexity, and the production of an economic surplus that may be invested in something other than food and shelter. Probably no one will question that mere existence can be sustained without much of what we take for granted in our lives.

But the matter is not so simple as this would suggest. Perhaps it is true that the simplest forms of life do not require libraries, but, as Ortega y Gasset reminds us, the survival of the human species does in certain ways depend on its ability to record and retain the lessons of the past. In support of this general viewpoint, recently historians have reminded us of the centrality of the role of libraries in the maintenance of civilization, noting that a decline in the fortunes of libraries is nearly always associated with a general decline in civilized activity.[3] Thus we can say that survival does require some accumulation of knowledge, and since most of us are not satisfied with mere survival, libraries quickly occupy a place much closer to the essential than at first appears.

Libraries are essential, then, to life as we consider it in all but its nastier and more brutish forms, for the knowledge record is really an adaptive mechanism, a means for more efficiently expanding and preserving our culture. The records of knowledge, and the places where we store them, may from certain points of view be exalted objects, but they are also among the most effective of tools for accomplishing practical goals, like claws that permit certain animals to climb or camouflage that enables others to escape their enemies. The record of knowledge is a force of considerable power and utility, for without it human groups are in the position of an individual suffering from amnesia—unable to remember past failures and successes, victims of slow trial and error.

The imaginative power of thought is the ability to project in the mind a set of possible solutions to problems, and it receives much of its input from the past, immediate and remote. And since it is impossible to think of the imagination without its own historical context, it is necessary for the imagination to take as its starting point the data of memory. An individual, even one of rare genius, remembers only a tiny slice of the past, and even a complex social group with many thousands of members can extend the reach of the individual only several generations back. With knowledge records, the reach of human memory encompasses all of human history, and the individual has the possibility of becoming the conscious product of that tradition. Thus the idea that libraries are "mere luxuries" is both misleading and false, for it does not really reflect what most of us consider essential to life as we know it.

This social function of expanding the collective memory places librarianship at the center of culture transmission. If we find, then, as Reeves did in his empirical study of work arrangements, that occupational institutions tend to control work settings, this is partly because these institutions are discharging critical social functions that cannot easily be left to chance or to an unregulated market of services. It makes more sense, in practical terms, to allow the occupation to control the work. The occupation, in Freidson's words, "succeeds in carving out a labor-market shelter."[4] This is, of course, true of a number of other occupations, including those that have never claimed to be professionally organized. What is distinctive about professional occupations is that the market shelter that helps to guarantee the delivery of the service is based on two types of higher education where two different types of knowledge are cultivated: liberal arts education and professional education.

Liberal Education as the Foundation for Professional Specialization

Liberal education is the intellectual and social foundation of professional work. Intellectually, it is the initial exposure to advanced systems of formal knowledge and systematic inquiry. Socially, it is the first phase of the market sheltering process outlined above, and is thus the first point in the process that determines who will have access to professional schools and thus eventually to professional occupations. In both the intellectual and social aspects, it performs an essential function of sorting or tracking persons into different walks of life.

What is true of the culture transmitting function of the library also holds, for very similar reasons, for liberal education. In a predominantly agricultural way of life, or in a culture founded on small-scale craft production, what we think of as a liberal education could hardly be defended as necessary to the formation of the worker. In these older types of societies, the mastery of the liberal arts appears of necessity as a mark of extreme privilege, restricted to the most elite strata. But in a society characterized by the complexity of the industrial division of labor, a corresponding complexity is increasingly required in the educational process to ensure the adequate preparation of certain types of workers.[5]

Thus even though the liberal component of higher education is frequently suspect in the world of practical affairs, it is nevertheless essential to that world for it lies at the heart of our way of life, with its emphasis on general literacy, mathematics, understanding of technology, and on the acquisition of certain broad intellectual problem-solving skills. The obvious fruits of specialization, in other words, depend on the ability to see the larger context within which the various specialties are situated. To be able to place the particular fact within a larger framework, and thus to discover some of the context giving it its meaning, is an ability that delivers urgent practical results as well as theoretical ones, for without it specialized work falls into triviality.

The liberal arts have long been recognized as essential to most if not all the professions, but they are even more central to librarianship than in other collegially controlled occupations. The reason is that librarians are much closer to the production and distribution of knowledge as a whole, and thus much closer to the problems of metascience than are most other professions. It is not nearly as necessary for a lawyer or a physician or an engineer to understand the general structure of knowledge that forms the larger context of the knowledge used in work routines. For librarians, this larger context is an essential feature of the specialized knowledge applied in the routine.

To facilitate the process of "recall"—extending Schopenhauer's metaphor—the librarian must be familiar with the general structure of knowledge. Given recent trends toward specialization throughout society, particularly in the areas of knowledge production, it makes sense to argue that librarians must also be familiar with a special discipline as well, for otherwise their grasp of the structure as a whole lacks the essential sense of knowledge as a cumulative growth of the larger from the smaller. This sense of the relation between the specialized and general areas of knowledge is first encountered in liberal arts education; it is there that the student first develops a sense of disciplines as parts in relation to a whole.[6]

Thus the kind of generalism librarians cultivate is really a development of the metascientific impulse within the contemporary liberal arts fields, and it requires advanced professional education to complete it. On the other hand, a puristic old-fashioned generalism is quite rightly rejected if it claims to support professionalized work arrangements. For this reason it is important not to assume that "specialists in generality"—or people who have not gone beyond the generalism of undergraduate education—are what is required in professional work. For if it is true that specialized work easily falls into triviality when not balanced by the metascientific impulse, it is also true that this older generalism is too superficial for contemporary purposes. What is important is the sense of the articulation of the structure of knowledge, or its "anatomy," in combination with its functional characteristics, or its "physiology." The role of specialization noted above suggests that one way to achieve this is to combine participation in knowledge production with the metascientific view of the whole. In these cases workers combine a general grasp of the structural and functional characteristics of knowledge with a more detailed grasp of how knowledge is produced in some special area.

With liberal education as a beginning, librarians and other information specialists often develop a measure of the expertise of the knowledge producer. One of the general patterns in most professional work finds the more advanced worker having more colleague than client contact. Indeed higher status work may be almost totally removed from clients; this is true in librarianship, at least where administration is the only path to advancement. The turn toward specialized competence in the production of knowledge is important because it increases colleague contact without requiring administrative advancement. And, of course, increased colleague contact supports control over work routines. In this way there is a direct link between the production of professional knowledge and the occupational control model.

The Culture of Inquiry

The importance of the liberal arts goes beyond this encounter with knowledge, and the first appreciation of its complexity. The student's contact with the special fields and the attempt to understand something of their relation to a whole is at the same time a contact with a new culture, a new sensibility. This is one of the foundations of later professional behavior. By observing professors, older students, or perhaps graduate students, students make contact with the culture of inquiry. It is a world in which one is not supposed to take everything for granted, and in this it is very different, at times extremely upsetting. One reason why the liberal arts are so important for later professional development is because this is where the first exposure to inquiry occurs. The importance of this initial contact is not so much with content as with style. As with the liberal arts, this phenomenon has both an intellectual and a social aspect, because the possession of this culture is part of the background needed to succeed in professional work; it, too, has something of a market-sheltering function.[7]

This culture of inquiry is the social cement that makes the various intellectual pursuits, as different as they are, part of the same set of social activities. In later professional life, its presence is essential for continuous individual development. The notion that "science" is a disciplined form of human inquiry is useful to consider here, for it reminds us that the contrasting methods of natural science and humanistic thought are united in this broader notion. The pursuit of almost any intellectual field by itself promotes certain habits of mind and general orientations that are essential to professional work, particularly librarianship. Examples are thinking in terms of evidence for or against certain points of view, the general habit of critical thinking, and an appreciation of the ambiguity inherent in any knowledge claim, whether a problem in textual criticism or a theory of cell structure. All of these are part of the knowledge-seeking orientation toward the world, part of the general culture of disciplined inquiry. They are particularly important in librarianship because it is so close to the processes of knowledge production and distribution. The intellectual and creative work that goes into the production of any record, regardless of discipline, includes both the intuitive power of mind and the more clearly rational and discursive power used to state claims and marshall evidence. The librarian's early exposure to the culture of inquiry is part of the background for understanding this.

PROFESSIONAL EDUCATION AND IDENTITY

Professional education, like liberal arts education and the culture of inquiry found there, continues the process of sheltering the market for those who have received the proper credentials and have appropriated the intellectual culture that comes with them. But, of course, it does much more than this. In addition to maintaining and transmitting the knowledge base of the occupation, it shapes the professional identity. There is a close relation between these two functions, for knowledge cannot be transmitted unless the student is properly formed to receive it. Some of this formation, as we have seen, occurs in liberal arts education, but some of it must be accomplished in the professional school itself. Accordingly, in this section, where we look at the controlling function of the library school, we focus not on the curriculum per se of professional education, but rather on the general aptitudes and orientations presupposed by any library school curriculum. By emphasizing these, library schools control the type of professional just entering the labor market.

We focus here on communicative interaction, quantitative and analytical ability, and the value orientations of intellectual freedom.

Language, Communication, Interaction

Even in the best of all possible worlds, broad general education as reflected in the liberal arts, a metascientific feeling for the structure of knowledge, and a major field of study are only the background of work. The educational process must also provide special skills and encourage the development of certain aptitudes. Among these are verbal skills, including a mastery of one's native language and as many others as possible. Even a slight acquaintance with foreign languages vastly increases one's ability to extend service beyond merely local interest, for natural languages are rooted in separate ways of life, with different approaches to knowledge and its production. A mastery of more than one language gives a unique breadth.

Aside from general linguistic competence, verbal skills are also crucial in the social psychology of librarianship, in communication, and interaction.[8] If one of the major tasks of the field is mediating between record and user, verbal skills are at the core of the mediating process. Robert S. Taylor has argued that the key activity of reference work is based on the interpretation of questions, and that questions are among the most complex types of human communication.[9] Of course, dealing with questions is only one type of communicative function, but librarians are all in one way or another concerned with some version of the kind of mediation between record and user that reference librarians specialize in. Librarians always work with real or hypothetical user-based questions before them, for the question is really the linguistic form that provides a starting place in determining the user's needs. The clarification of the query draws upon the active use of the imagination discussed in Chapter 2. Thus the ability to deal with complex questions is based on the ability to articulate one's own questions, and is rooted in the free play of the imagination. This is not unique to professional work, still less to librarianship, for it is a general characteristic of the more complex forms of intellectual labor. But it is an essential feature of professional work in libraries. The first step in encouraging its development is in the school, in the recruitment of a certain type of student, in contact with teachers and peers, and in promoting the problem-solving habit of mind.

Quantitative and Analytical Ability

The need for quantitative skills in librarianship is and probably will remain controversial, if only because, as a matter of fact, librarians commonly have humanistic backgrounds. But there are other reasons. One is that communicative interaction and interpretation are so central to much of the work that it is natural to recruit people from humanistic fields. It is only rarely that people trained in the sciences can match the communicative skills of humanists. Another is that the humanistic tradition is much more closely allied to the library as a social institution than are the scientific, technical, or purely vocational traditions, and thus libraries, particularly the larger and more important ones, tend to favor that tradition. Still another reason is that users interested in history, the humanities, and the arts are more frequent users of libraries than are scientists, not only because they are more bookish but because the nature of their information need is more easily satisfied by traditional collections.

But even though there are good reasons why librarians are often humanists, this creates a problem for the schools, for librarianship now requires quantitative skills in addition to, rather than instead of, communicative skills. Analytical skills, although not necessarily numerical, are closely related. The particular forms this problem takes in professional education lie with selection and re-cruitment of students, and with the processes of self-formation that occur in library education. Clearly, in a society where the "two cultures" of humanism and science are often at odds, this is not an easy combination to find. Library schools seem at present to be following two strategies. Some try to capitalize on the strengths of the existing population, hoping to extract the metascientific potential from these backgrounds, and expose students increasingly to quanti-tative or analytical methods.[10] Others so strongly slant the curriculum in the direction of information science that other viewpoints are more or less excluded; in these programs there is a cult of quantitative tough mindedness. Both strategies attempt to preserve the market shelter by transmitting new types of knowledge and by directly influencing the worker in the early stages of identity formation.

Certainly this much is clear: an essential feature of the professional identity of the librarian is the ability to abstract from the concrete, to ignore the immediate quality long enough to see the abstract pattern among the details. Mediation among records and users requires, in addition to communication, the ability to abstract the formal properties of documents from their contents. The use of the artificial languages associated with quantitative skills liberates us from the concrete; and, of course, these artificial languages are essential to the organization, storage, and retrieval of documents—all those areas, in other words, in which the interpretation of the content of the record is secondary to the organization of bodies of records by formal characteristics.

The importance of the quantitative—in this sense of abstracting from the concrete—is not new, but it is more central to professional work as automation advances. Computerized cataloging and computer-assisted literature searching, for example, are two of the more recent aspects of the general spread of automation in libraries. For the last ten years most announcements of professional positions in libraries insist on some familiarity with machine-readable records, and the artificial languages of logic and algebra are implicit in the formulas for subject searching used in various online systems. And citation indexing, although it represents a great departure from semantic approaches to retrieval, still relies on the ability to ignore the content in favor of formal properties.[11]

Values, Professional Education, and Control

We have noted the value dimension in connection with ethics codes in the trait theory, and in light of C. P. Snow's two cultures thesis.[12] In the trait theory, the ethics code rests on commitments to free inquiry, freedom of expression, freedom to read, and the corresponding rights of clients to exercise these freedoms. Of librarianship's two cultures, we argued that the value dimension of the knowledge base displays the same range of depth and complexity found in the cognitive pole. But when we look at values in the context of social control over work routines, we see a somewhat different picture.

In practical terms, a certain value orientation ensures a general similarity of outlook and thus reinforces the cohesion of the group. More immediately, it protects professional practice from client control. The occupation does not only need to articulate such commitments, it needs even more to be able to ensure that the individuals in practice share them, and this is much more difficult. It is partly a matter of selection and recruitment, and partly of the formation of a professional self with suitable value orientations. As we have seen, librarianship places a strong emphasis on the values of traditional liberalism. This reflects to some degree the bourgeois origins of modern libraries and modern professional work in libraries. Libraries as we know them, with their missions of service to diverse populations of users, are among the more significant products of the knowledge explosions of the last three hundred years. And because much of that knowledge was produced by people who believed strongly in toleration and free inquiry, the social institutions that arose to control it reflect a similar ideological orientation. Thus if librarians tend to be more liberal in their social and political values than other professionals, this is not surprising. It is part of the ideological background of the work.

But there is more to this than ideology, for libraries and librarians are subjected to intense pressures of censorship. Particularly in public, school, and smaller academic libraries, work routines are sometimes brought to a complete stop.[13] This represents an attempt at one of the purest forms of client control. There are several ways that professional education uses value orientations to prevent this from happening. By presupposing liberal arts education as background, the professional school requires an initial openness to the norms of free inquiry. Thus it begins the process by making sure that only a certain type of individual comes to it in the first place. Second, there are courses in intellectual freedom that build on this foundation and introduce students to some of the complex social, legal, and philosophical background of censorship and intellectual freedom. Third, the culture of the professional school itself is strongly prejudiced in the direction of the classic values of liberalism. There is, in short, a cultural homogeneity that strongly discourages deviation from liberal values.

THE ASSOCIATION AND STANDARD SETTING

The concern with value is also very evident in the American Library Association's Codes of Ethics, which establish standards for professional behavior and the protection of client interests, and in the work of its Intellectual Freedom Committee.[14] It is noteworthy, in connection with the concerns of occupational control that the code mentions the essential confidential relationship between the user and the library. This confidentiality is one of the more important marks of collegial control, even though violations occur occasionally in all professions. A key point of difference between the normatively and structurally founded forms of occupational control emerges: in structurally controlled professions, the associations typically exercise the right to revoke the professional status of code violators. With its predominantly normatively based control, librarianship does not do this.[15]

There are many other areas in which the ALA has engaged in standard setting activities. Materials selectors and collection development librarians, for example, have for some time relied on selection tools and generic standards for collections policy formulated by the Resources and Technical Services Division. The same is true for reference librarians, who have developed standards under the auspices of the Reference and Adult Services Division.[16] These specialized forms of standard setting are crucial in determining how work will be done in certain areas. Underlying these special forms, however, are standards that cut across the specialized functions. We focus here on one generic area of standard setting in which the ALA has attempted to control the way work is done in libraries. By supporting specific educational qualifications, especially the Master's degree, as standard credentials for entering professionals, the association illustrates the market-sheltering mechanism of control examined above in the context of liberal education and professional education.

Education and Labor Power Policy: ALA Statements 1948–84

The ALA has consistently provided definitions of work that include at least three basic elements: professional, paraprofessional, and clerical support. This is apparent in a series of statements drafted over the last forty years.[17] By looking at the three levels in relation to each other, we have an idea of the implicit official definition of professional work and can see that it has been relatively consistent over time.

Educational qualifications have played a central role in distinguishing professionals from one another as well as from other types of workers. The insistence on formal professional training goes back at least to the influential Williamson Report of 1923; by 1948 the ALA was recommending the Master's degree and strongly encouraging doctoral programs.[18] Later statements, for example in 1970, affirm the importance of the liberal arts background for both professionals and assistants, adopting the Master's degree as official policy for professional workers.[19] The 1970 statement leaves open the possibility that a claim to professional status might be based on expertise in "some other field," but this seems pro forma: almost all professional positions in libraries require at least the M.L.S. (There are, however, continuing challenges to this requirement, both from within the ALA and from a combination of external social and legal forces.)[20]

The 1970 policy proposal draws a key distinction in the task domains. Professional work is contrasted with "routine applications of rules," on the one hand— the task area of the library assistant, or as it is sometimes called, the library technician. On the other, it contrasts with "supportive work," the domain of clerical workers. Terminology varies, of course, and it would be useful to know in more detail whether or not there is any real difference between a "technician" and an "assistant." The community college programs that call themselves courses in "library technology" suggest that, whatever the title, paraprofessional work is strongly connected to the operation of computerized bibliographic utilities at the "routine task and rule" level: circulation systems, copy cataloging, and bibliographic checking are three of the more obvious examples. But in some cases these functions are performed by support workers, particularly in smaller or medium-size libraries. In still other cases—particularly very small libraries— these functions, along with all professional ones, are carried out by a professional.

In the professional worker category, the 1970 statement—again building on 1948—draws further distinctions between types of professionals, mainly to account for the assumption of managerial or administrative authority in complex library organizations. The "senior librarian" requires educational qualifications beyond those outlined for professionals, although the kind of qualifications is not specified. The library administrator should be recruited only from the senior librarian category.

Even if the official policy on the Master's degree did not come until later, the themes of autonomy and authority as based on advanced professional education are crucial threads linking both statements.[21] Since the 1970 statement builds on the 1948 statement of the task levels, we can see immediately that the claim for autonomy is enduring; if support staff "routinely apply rules," then professionals must be the ones who formulate the rules they apply. Not, of course, in the sense that individual professionals make up the rules as they go along—though that lamentable situation may exist in certain cases—but rather in the sense that the rules that constitute the detailed versions of the profession's standards are the results of a corporate effort. The occupational group, in other words, is the source of the rules and the interpretations necessary to use them.

Before 1970, the official position equivocates on educational qualifications in certain ways. What body of knowledge should the professional master? Library and information science, or "some other field"? As far as standards for work routines are concerned, the official position is clear enough, but it says nothing about the relationships between standards, educational qualifications, and the kinds of knowledge that such qualifications ideally represent. What has happened, as a matter of fact, leaving policy aside for the moment, is that younger librarians in many types of libraries must have educational qualifications in at least two fields: the first is some recognized version of library science, library service, information science, or some combination; the second varies with the type of library and nature of the specialty, and includes such diverse areas as subject specialization, teacher certification, computer programming, systems analysis, media services, archival management, and documentation. This is in part merely a reflection of the great diversity of library types, a diversity among types of knowledge records, and a corresponding diversity of appropriate work roles.

The 1970 statement equivocates in another interesting way on the issue of educational qualifications. Although it very clearly recommends academic preparation as the best means of initial tracking, it also mentions the possibility of formal examinations as a substitute for such preparation. This seems not to be taken seriously in many actual work situations, although it does exist. Even where there are such examinations, the actual power of the degree requirement is considerable.[22] Thus while the ALA's official statements up to 1970 are qualified, support for the knowledge base through support of the educational program is very clear.

In any case none of this reflects negatively on the association's commitment to maintaining occupational cohesion through collegial standard setting. As Reeves points out, both the 1948 and the 1970 statements clearly support the idea that librarians are "the only source of formal policy, guidelines, and regulations," and the two statements also agree that supervisory authority is a unique professional function.[23] In the key area of selection and reference, for example, priority is clearly with selection, which sets the general boundaries for reference work. The reason is that selection is a purely professional task, whereas reference is typically a mixture of professional and nonprofessional duties.[24]

Since 1970 there has been a change of emphasis in ALA statements, a shift toward more explicitly political action as support for control over work routines.[25] The association now urges lobbying, public relations campaigns, and the marketing of professional services as additional means of preserving control. But the basic definitions of professional and nonprofessional work have remained.[26] In any case, these changes are quite general and affect most occupations, including most collegially controlled ones. As anyone who reads the newspaper can clearly see, many professional groups now advertise or otherwise engage in overt competition for public attention, or attempt to directly influence the political process through means once thought "unprofessional."

Most recently, however, political awareness has taken a fresh turn, as the ALA has shifted its attention to defending the M.L.S., thought to be under attack as a minimum qualification for professional work. Beginning in the recession years of the 1970s and continuing into the early 1980s, various challenges have emerged to the M.L.S. as the "industry standard." These have come from various quarters: fiscal austerity in the federal government, the increase in unaccredited programs along with the closing of some accredited programs, the merging in some universities of the library school with other university departments or schools, encroachment from outsiders using the courts, and others.[27] But there is another source of concern here also, not so much from a sense of being attacked or challenged as from a realization of basic structural change in the nature of professional work in libraries and elsewhere in our society. This concern has to do with the fact that it no longer makes sense to require the M.L.S. for certain types of work in libraries, particularly in circulation, reserve, interlibrary loan, and related areas.[28]

FORMALIZATION AND DIFFERENTIATION OF CONTROL

Much of the above nicely illustrates some themes in the recent study of patterns of occupational control in collegial groups. It has been observed that as professional work comes to be situated routinely in complex organizations, there is a strong tendency for "differentiation" and "formalization" to occur.[29] Because the work itself and the organization where it is performed are much more complex than in the past, specialization within the occupation creates subgroups or subtypes of workers; administrators, once recruited informally from the ranks of practitioners, tend to be drawn into a separate pattern of professional development, with contrasting paths of entry, advancement, and separation. For example, administrators in major research libraries may look to formal continuing education programs, such as the Council on Library Resources academic library management internships, as places to recruit new people. The same forces that bring about this differentiating of subgroups within the original whole also require an increasing reliance on formal as opposed to informal means of control. In addition to the development of an administrative elite, there is also an increased reliance on educational qualifications, educational performance, licensing bodies, and formal certification programs, all of which reinforce the formalizing tendency and advance the idea of a "rational" approach to delivering professional services. The ALA policy statements on labor power reflect this tendency clearly because they recognize the "splitting off" of the administrative subgroup from the rest of the occupation.

Challenges to control are, of course, an old story, for professional dominance has in one way or another always been challenged. In any case some of the current concern with the M.L.S. can be seen as a special case of either forces of "deprofessionalization" or "mediation," depending on interpretation.[30] We need only point out here that these concerns are not necessarily evidence for loss of collegial control. The challenge to the M.L.S. is probably related to a current popular mood; there are forces everywhere challenging professional authority in various fields. It is thus only natural that credentialing, with its frequent reliance on educational qualifications, should come under fire. Whether or not we are witnessing deprofessionalization or mediation of control depends on the challenge and where it is coming from, among other things. The attack on the M.L.S., if that is what it is, may be rooted in the current concern with "competency" in work; the notion that degrees and other formal qualifications need to reflect actual work requirements rather than general ideas developed in schools by professional educators. The situation is inherently ambiguous, for it depends on who is defining the competencies. Of course, one can take the very idea of "competence" very broadly or very narrowly. And so the debate continues.

CONCLUSION

Occupations are situated in a network of larger social forces. This is partly a matter of fact and also because they deliver essential services. The control that their institutions exercise over work is, in other words, part of a larger pattern of social and cultural activity. In this sense, we can say that work arrangements are ultimately controlled by society, working through the special institutions of the occupation. This does not necessarily mean official regulation, but rather a more pervasive and ultimately more effective kind of social regulation. It is, as noted in Chapter 4, a mix between the official and the unofficial, the structural and the normative. In some cases the broader type of social control is highly restrictive and legalistic; in others more of an informal consensus. The point is that librarianship, like many other types of work, is too important to be left entirely to the practitioners. It must in some way answer to basic social needs.

By maintaining access to knowledge records, librarians participate in the production and reproduction of culture. The general social function of the library links the occupation to a wider set of social needs. Like a number of professional occupations, librarianship has a strong connection with higher education, the liberal arts, and the "culture of inquiry" that flourishes there. This is true in two ways: first, because professional education presupposes the liberal arts, and second, because the professional school itself is located in the university. But while other occupations have this connection also, librarianship's association with knowledge records gives it a special form. The applied metascience that makes up a significant part of librarianship's knowledge base is much more intimately related to the production and distribution of knowledge than is true for other occupations. And the ideological stress on freedom of access to information makes this connection with knowledge even stronger.

The social background of control finds its link to work through the two major institutions of the occupation, the professional school and the association. The school presupposes the social necessity of reproducing culture and the liberal arts background and takes them as its starting points. Charged with the formation of the occupational identity and the transmission of the knowledge base, it stresses communicative interaction, quantitative/analytical orientations, and value (intellectual freedom, and so on). The associations, as noted in the Reeves study, are largely concerned with standard setting. Because the standard setting activity includes the definition of the professional worker, expressed in generic job descriptions, the association also has a role to play in the formation of professional identity. This role is expressed in the ALA work analysis statements presented here.

NOTES

1. For example, Wilfred Lancaster, "Whither Libraries? Wither Libraries?" *College and Research Libraries* 39, 5 (September 1978): 345–57. Lancaster shifts his focus somewhat from the institution to the institutionally situated professional in a later essay: "Future Librarianship: Implications for Library and Information Science Education," *Library Trends* 32, 3 (Winter 1984): 337–48.

2. Schopenhauer's observation has been used by many writers, including Georg Leyh, *Die Bildung des Bibliothekars* (Copenhagen: Munskgaard, 1952), p. 11, and Jose Ortega y Gasset, "The Mission of the Librarian," *Antioch Review* 21 (Summer 1961): 133–54.

3. Ortega y Gasset, "The Mission of the Librarian," p. 150; on the relation between libraries and civilization, see Immanuel Wallerstein and John Frank Stephens, *Libraries and Our Civilizations. A Report Prepared for the Governor of the State of New York*, Governor's Conference on Libraries, June 1978.

4. Eliot Freidson, *Professional Powers: A Study of the Institutionalization of Formal Knowledge* (Chicago: University of Chicago Press, 1986), p. 59.

5. The analysis of social class and social stratification that is presupposed by these developments is well beyond the scope of the present discussion. We mention this because there are many other factors responsible for the spread of mass higher education than the requirements of the occupational structure. See, for example, Harry Braverman, *Labor and Monopoly Capital: The Degradation of Work in the Twentieth Century* (New York: Monthly Review Press, 1974), pp. 439–40; also Samuel Bowles and Herbert Gintis,

Schooling in Capitalist America: Educational Reform and the Contradictions of Economic Life (New York: Basic Books, 1976).

6. This encounter in liberal arts education is essential for any later appreciation of recent advances in the study of how knowledge grows. In the last twenty-five years historians of science, sociologists of science, librarians, and information scientists have built contemporary models of the growth and development of human knowledge that avoid the older assumptions of simple linear "progress." See, for example, Thomas Kuhn, *The Structure of Scientific Revolutions* (Chicago: University of Chicago Press, 1962); Imre Lakatos and Alan Musgrave, eds. *Criticism and the Growth of Knowledge* (Cambridge: Cambridge University Press, 1970); Paul Feyerabend, *Against Method: Outline of an Anarchistic Theory of Knowledge* (Atlantic Highlands, NJ: Humanities Press, 1975); Don R. Swanson, "Libraries and the Growth of Knowledge," *Library Quarterly* 50 (January 1980): 112–34. In particular, Kuhn's notion of "paradigm" has been very widely discussed. Even more recently, historians of science and technology, working along with librarians and information scientists, have explored some of the same territory in an attempt to provide models of literature growth that are loosely based on the same rejection of the assumption of linear development. A very ingenious model, for example, was developed by Derek de Solla Price, based on the comparison of bodies of literature to islands and continents. In Price's model, newly created bodies of literature are "islands," while the more established fields acquire a massive "continental" quality. In some cases, continents are formed by a gradual accretion of islands into a mass. What began as an isolated spot in an ocean of ignorance becomes a settled territory occupied by many researchers; for example, Derek de Solla Price, "Development and Structure of the Biomedical Literature," *Coping with the Biomedical Literature: A Primer for the Scientist and the Clinician*, ed. Kenneth S. Warren (New York: Praeger, 1981), pp. 3–16. For a more recent statement and application of the geographical metaphor, see Henry Small and Eugene Garfield, "The Geography of Science: Disciplinary and National Mappings," *Journal of Information Science* 11 (1985): 147–59. For example, Shakespeare scholarship, diplomatic history, and cardiology are vast continental masses; while historical sociology, health psychology, and psychoimmunology are still only sparsely populated islands. The game of discovering where the continents are going to form is part of the intellectual adventure of librarianship.

7. This connection between the culture of inquiry and questions of market-sheltering and social class is explored in Eliot Freidson, *Professional Powers*, pp. 44–49.

8. Florence De Hart, *The Librarian's Psychological Commitments: Human Relations in Librarianship* (Westport, CT: Greenwood Press, 1979).

9. Robert S. Taylor, "Question Negotiation and Information Seeking in Libraries," *College and Research Libraries* 29 (May 1968): 178–79.

10. Some educators recognize, for example, that traditional methods in the social sciences have undergone considerable transformation. Historical studies are no longer one-sidedly qualitative, nor are other social sciences nearly so historically naive as they once were. For a discussion of the relationship between sociology and history, which explores how the two fields have benefited from a cross-fertilization of quantitative and qualitative methods of inquiry, see Patrick Wilson, *Second Hand Knowledge: An Inquiry into Cognitive Authority* (Westport, CT: Greenwood Press, 1983), pp. 96ff.

11. Self-formation is not restricted to practical techniques. The intellectual foundations here include set theory, Boolean algebra, and truth-functional logic. All of these provide methods of dealing with the formal properties of generic universes of relationships:

relationships among propositions, terms, numbers, and among domains of unspecified entities. Clearly anyone who is uncomfortable with the algebraic notion of the variable—who cannot grasp the idea of using known values to search for unknowns—will have trouble doing computerized searching. The series of discoveries made over a period of years spanning the midnineteenth to the early twentieth centuries leading to the insight that mathematics and logic can each be derived from a more primitive system of rules for pure combinations is thus central to the work of the online searcher. Naturally the use of the computer on a practical level does not require explicit reference to this intellectual history. But it was made possible by this history, and that leads us to suspect that developments occurring at the present time may have a similar effect on later generations of searchers. For a general theoretical statement written in the early period of online searching, see Allen Kent, *Information Analysis and Retrieval* (New York: Becker and Hayes, 1971), pp. 166ff.

12. Chapters 2 and 4, respectively.

13. David Berninghausen, *The Flight from Reason: Essays on Intellectual Freedom in the Academy, the Press, and the Library* (Chicago: American Library Association, 1975); and also by the same author, "The History of the ALA Intellectual Freedom Committee," *Wilson Library Bulletin* 27 (June 1953): 813–17; "Teaching a Commitment to Intellectual Freedom," *Library Journal* 92 (October 1967): 3601–05.

14. For a recent comprehensive survey covering the period between 1929 and 1981, see Jonathan A. Lindsey and Ann E. Prentice, *Professional Ethics and Librarians* (Phoenix, AZ: Oryx Press, 1985).

15. This was proposed by Clarence Graham in 1950. David K. Berninghausen, School of Library Science, University of Minnesota, to author, personal communication of October 15, 1979.

16. The Resources and Technical Services Division of the ALA is producing a series of selection tools that will set standards for some time to come: see, for example, Patricia McClung, ed., *Selection of Library Materials in the Humanities, Social Sciences, and the Sciences* (Chicago: American Library Association, 1985); and Beth J. Shapiro, ed., *Selection of Library Materials in Applied and Interdisciplinary Fields* (Chicago: American Library Association, 1987).

17. See *A Descriptive List of Professional and Nonprofessional Duties in Libraries* (Chicago: American Library Association, 1948); and, some twenty years later, "Library Education and Manpower: American Library Association Policy Proposal," prepared by Lester Asheim, *American Libraries* 1 (April 1970): pp. 341ff. Reeves points out that the Canadian Library Association accepted the same basic viewpoint in 1972. See *Librarians as Professionals: The Occupation's Impact on Library Work Arrangements* (Lexington, MA: Lexington Books, 1980), p. 21.

18. For a historical overview, see William Z. Nasri, "Education in Librarian and Information Science: Education for Librarianship," *Encyclopedia of Library and Information Science* (New York: Marcel Dekker, 1968).

19. Reeves, *Librarians as Professionals*, p. 20.

20. Pauline Wilson, "The ALA, the MLS, and Professional Employment," *American Libraries* 14 (December 1983): 743; also by Pauline Wilson, "The ALA, the MLS, and Professional Employment: An Observer's Field Guide to the Issues," *American Libraries* 15, 8 (September 1984): 563–66. See also Keith Cottam, "Minimum Qualifications and the Law: The Issue Ticks Away for Librarians," *American Libraries* 11, 5 (May 1980): 280–81.

21. Reeves, *Librarians as Professionals*, p. 22.

22. And in any case one can hardly imagine the imposition of an examination in any of these cases. The Medical Library Association does have a certification program based on a standard "experience and training rating" type of examination, but examinees normally must have already spent two years in professional practice before taking the exam—at least to receive "full" as opposed to "provisional" certification—and thus the certification procedure in effect if not as a matter of policy presupposes the M.L.S.

23. Reeves, p. 21.

24. Ibid., p. 25.

25. Ibid., p. 31.

26. "ALA Goals and Objectives: Revised Draft," *American Libraries* 6 (1975): 39–41.

27. Pauline Wilson, "Professionalism: Focus on the Basics," an unpublished address delivered at the Graduate School of Library Science at the University of Michigan, May 1985, pp. 9ff. The author thanks Pauline Wilson for providing him with a printed text of the speech.

28. Keith Cottam, "The ALA, the MLS, and Professional Employment," *Employee Selection and Minimum Qualifications for Librarians*, ed. Keith Cottam (Chicago: American Library Association, 1984).

29. Eliot Freidson, "The Changing Nature of Professional Control," *Annual Review of Sociology* 10 (1984): 13ff.

30. See Chapter 3.

6

The Trick Question: Thinking Through the Occupation/Profession Debate

THREE ASSUMPTIONS

The discerning reader will notice that something is missing; in fact, it is omitted by design. But it cannot be altogether ignored, if only because so much of the literature on the library profession has centered everything around it. This is the question that has fascinated some sociologists and many librarians: is librarianship a profession? If no attempt has been made to answer the question, it is because there is something peculiar about it. What is peculiar is not what it asks, but what it assumes. Before granting the question a place in this discussion, we look at three crucial assumptions.

In the first place, the question assumes that we know what a profession is. Second, it assumes that an occupation can be defined neatly enough to make a comparison between it and our knowledge of what a profession is. We are not justified, however, in making either assumption, for the question of what a profession is has proved to be a continuing and open one. Sociologists, historians, and others make new discoveries about the world of work, the role of professional work in that world, and about the relationship between work and human culture generally. There seems to be no such thing as a single, unambiguous definition of anything as complex as "profession"; rather, it is a continuing task of intellectual interpretation. In the case of the second assumption, the issues of measurement have never been satisfactorily resolved, and so it would be extremely difficult, perhaps unlikely, to settle the methodological problems in the measurement of occupations against standard definitions. But although there is no single answer to the question of what is a profession, there are many useful and interesting ones. Beyond these qualified answers lie only more interpretation and more debate; and this, in any complex and interesting intellectual question, is precisely as it should be.[1]

The third assumption is the idea that an occupation and a profession are objects from the same general class of things. And, of course, for the trait theory and the functionalist view, this is the case. However, this idea fails to distinguish between an occupation—a type of social group defined by common tasks and routines in the workplace—and the strategies that occupations use to exercise control over work routines. Clearly, a social group and a strategy for control are different types of things. If we think of these strategies for control as professions, we cannot say that *occupation* and *profession* refer to the same general type of thing. On the other hand, a collegially controlled occupation can be meaningfully put in the same category as a managerially controlled occupation, or indeed, a client controlled occupation. If we think in general terms of all occupations, we can compare different forms of control as types of things drawn from the same category: collegial control, mediated control, client control, and so on.

It is worth noting that even if we reject the recent tendency to analyze work in terms of control—even if we insist, after all that has been said, that the trait theory or the functionalist approach is still the best tool to use in understanding the professions—it would still be true that the whole question of control is best addressed separately. No description of a collegially controlled work group is complete without a separate consideration of these mechanisms. In this sense the distinction between occupational groups and strategies for control is valid independently of our preference in theories.

THE OCCUPATION/PROFESSION DEBATE

Nonetheless, the question is still asked—is librarianship a profession?—without regard for the three assumptions. And it is worthwhile to see why this kind of approach should be rejected. William J. Goode's much discussed and reprinted paper, one of many attempts to answer the question in its simplest form, states a strong case against librarianship: for Goode, the answer is no.[2] But even if the answer had been yes, the conclusion would have been equally suspect, for it is still based on the reductionist attempt to answer the question without consideration of its assumptions.

Goode's case is centered on four basic points in the definition of a profession: an accepted body of abstract knowledge forming the basis of practice, theoretical contributions to the knowledge base by practitioners, legitimate monopoly over the knowledge, and professional/client relations. The library profession, according to Goode, falls short in each category. Library science, he argues, is not a well-defined field of inquiry. Nor do librarians concern themselves greatly with making scholarly contributions to their field, a claim that is supported by some evidence. For example, Elizabeth Stone's 1969 research revealed that significant numbers of academic librarians are not involved in research and do not stay current in the literature of their fields.[3] Goode concludes that an underdeveloped knowledge base, coupled with low commitment to scholarly work, stimulates a cycle of occupational underdevelopment. Third, librarians have no special control over the uses of their knowledge in the way in which doctors and lawyers, for example, have exclusive rights to certain uses of medical and legal knowledge. Finally, librarians do not enjoy the privileges of control of the client. The librarian, unlike the doctor or lawyer, has no special authority over the client and does not dictate the correct view of the client's need.

Critique of the Occupation/Profession Debate: Theoretical Issues

It should be clear that this reductionist approach is open to a number of very telling theoretical objections. It relies, in effect, on a combined version of the trait and functionalist models. It does not even ask, let alone attempt to answer, any of the important questions on occupational control that have been raised in the more recent work on the professions. In Reeves's terms, it relies on a purely structuralist interpretation of occupations; the role of normative order in occupational groups is unrecognized. Thus while Goode is correct in saying that librarianship does not involve any legal monopoly over knowledge, this is true for many other professions, including the academic, and is not at all central to whether or not any given occupation is a profession. What is most important, and what Goode does not recognize, is the existence of a social or cultural monopoly—a normatively upheld control over certain types of knowledge. This normative control is based on the period of training and specialization, the complexity of the knowledge base, standards set by the central association, shared orientations among practitioners, and, of course, on the inability of outsiders to provide the service for themselves. That legal sanctions are not involved tells us only that librarianship shows the normative pattern of authority and control. Legally, anyone who wants to may engage in curriculum analysis, write on formal logic, teach organic chemistry, or practice librarianship. To conclude from this that none of these is professional is obviously to ignore the normative sanctions governing all of them.

But even in structurally professionalized groups, formal regulation is seldom sufficient to enforce controls on social behavior, and is generally supported by informal consensus. Structural authority, in other words, depends on normative authority for its foundation. Indeed, without normative authority, structural versions of control are costly, extremely time-consuming, and cumbersome to maintain. Even in a highly regulated work situation, the impossibility of constant legal oversight of professional behavior requires a strong normative foundation. The same point holds, in fact, throughout the world of routine social behavior; if structural controls were required to enforce compliance, social order could hardly exist in the first place. Most people stop at red lights; most lawyers avoid conflicts of interest; most librarians do not engage in flagrant forms of censorship or freely reveal the identities of library users on circulation records. Most behavior, in other words, in and out of the workplace falls within acceptable limits without invoking laws or other official rules of conduct. The reason is that most people have internalized general norms of conduct that reflect a shared sense of correct behavior in that situation.

The dependence of structural authority on normative foundations is in fact, as the above parallel suggests, only a special case of a general pattern of social order. Routine behavior at all levels always depends on informally shared norms of conduct; the explicit mechanisms of regulation that sometimes exist along with them are derivative. One of the best-known examples is in the area of contract, but it applies generally to any area in which people make rational agreements. Contractual agreements are built on a foundation or assumption of basic trust, which recognizes the internalization of common norms as the basis of behavior. It is only when the trust is violated, or when the social consequences of violation are considered particularly great, that structural forms of control need to be articulated.[4] Writers who attempt to describe professional work in terms of structural control alone are thus missing the normative foundation, and they make much the same mistake that earlier social thinkers made when they tried to account for all human behavior in terms of rational agreements based on perceived utility or self-interest.

This is not to suggest that the structural element is unimportant, for it is a reflection of a deep-seated social judgment. In occupations where the structural element predominates, there is an implicit evaluation of the immediate importance of that occupation. Thus, among the professions, medicine and law show high levels of structural control because we judge the provision of these services to be particularly crucial, in a very direct way, to our health and safety. The consequences of allowing such work to go unregulated are too great. But notice also that the structural foundation is equally important in a number of occupations where there has never been any claim to professional status, such as construction, plumbing, electrical contracting, and various other kinds of highly skilled craft labor, where the consequences of poor service are direct threats to our health and safety. What this should tell us is that certain occupations, some professional and some not—that is, some collegially controlled and some not—provide services of more direct relevance to our immediate well-being than do other occupations. It does not give us a test that can be used to separate professional from nonprofessional occupations. And, of course, it would be absurd to argue that just because a certain service is more central to our health or safety that it is for *that* reason more clearly "professional" than some other type of service.

The same general idea also applies to Goode's last point, the authority of the professional over the client. In medicine and law this is legally sanctioned, or so the argument goes. We know now, as Goode perhaps cannot be expected to have known at the time, that this view of the power of the professional over the client is, at least from the present standpoint, exaggerated. Indeed, for all types of professional work, the older idea of individual autonomy has been gradually supplemented by mediated forms of control, or in some cases by the gradual coming of client control. In sum, there are a great many forces that now act as barriers to unchecked professional power. But even so, professionals still have considerable resources for defining the nature of their services and the manner in which such services will be delivered, and this is due to strong normative foundations, which persist even in situations where structural authority has gradually weakened. In other words, the social sanctions one finds in collegially controlled occupations are, in their own way, just as strong and accomplish similar goals. For example, when a knowledge base develops continually, becomes more refined and complex, and is perceived as in some way indispensable to the public good, the importance of the occupation increases, without any help from the law.

Historical parallels are useful here. Not so long ago—a generation or two at most—many of the social sciences were regarded as stepchildren of more established disciplines. Sociology, for example, was originally practiced and developed by persons trained in other fields: Herbert Spencer was an engineer, Auguste Comte and Durkheim philosophers, Weber an economic historian and legal scholar, W. I. Thomas a professor of literature, and Albion Small a historian—a highly diverse group of founders for a discipline with a much more precisely defined focus today. In its early days American sociology was also full of clergymen looking for tools to accomplish good works through benevolent social engineering, and the line between sociology as a research profession and sociology as an applied concern was elusive. Indeed, these two strains are still present in the modern version of the discipline. But over time, the development of the knowledge base of the field, the splitting of sociology from social work and anthropology, the acceptance of sociology in the major graduate schools, and the recruitment and training of a core of teachers and scholars gradually changed all this.[5] The history of academic psychology shows some similarity; even as late as the turn of the century, before the experimental method had taken hold, psychology was derived largely from philosophy, and many academic departments included religion as well. Such examples from the history of the academic professions should make us suspect any theory of the professions that puts an exclusive emphasis on the structural aspect of occupational organization. Perhaps even more so, it should alert us to the fact that occupations change considerably over periods of time.[6]

Critique of the Occupation/Profession Debate: Empirical Issues

Aside from the theoretical problems, the attempt to deny librarianship professional status is suspect on empirical grounds as well. Even if it were justifiable to take "traits" as indicators of professionalism, we could not on that basis exclude librarians from the professional occupations. We cannot look at every trait, but consider as an example the building of the knowledge base through contributions to the literature. The alleged fact that practitioners do not contribute to research literatures cannot be held against any occupation, for it is normally teachers and scholars who carry out this function and not practitioners. Practitioner literature is normally characterized by a mix of policy and case reporting, and this is true not only of librarianship but of law and medicine as well.[7] Thus empirical findings showing that practitioners do not contribute significantly to research literature cannot be used as evidence against a claim for professional status. In fact, however, there are some findings more recent than Stone's 1969 study indicating that in librarianship there is significant research and publication activity among practitioners. A 1980 study showed that over 40 percent of surveyed libraries required librarians with faculty status to publish. Even including nonfaculty librarians, the figure is, at 15 percent, high for a group in which most hold full-year contracts. Other studies confirm that in comparison with other occupations, working librarians make substantial contributions to the research literature.[8,9]

What does this newer evidence tell us? It is not easy to evaluate, but it seems to indicate that in certain areas of librarianship the traditional division of labor between practitioners and scholar/educators does not hold, for here is a field in which practitioners *do* make substantial contributions to the literature. By itself, however, this does not answer the question of whether librarianship is a professional field. It is really not clearly related to that question at all. It may suggest that there needs to be a greater emphasis on research on the part of library educators. Quite apart from professionalization, it gives grounds for optimism about the state of the field, since it is relatively unusual to find practitioners showing such a high interest in research and publication.

CHARACTERISTICS OF THE RESEARCH LITERATURE

The argument, as we have seen, rests partly on negative assessments of the knowledge base as reflected in the literature, but when we look closely, we find that such arguments never really show an effort to describe the research literature of the field. Instead they substitute impressionistic judgments. In part this is because the necessary studies are relatively recent, but it is also an indication of the tendency to simply assume that the literature of the field is not really a bona fide research literature. The prevailing assumption is that of a purely anecdotal body of work. Of course, there is a substantial element of anecdotal material in the literature of librarianship, as there is in the case-oriented literature of law and medicine, among other occupational groups. But this alone cannot be taken to prove that the literature or its affiliated knowledge base is not to be taken seriously, or that it cannot support the work of professionals. But since this is clearly the implication of Goode's argument, we should examine the literature to see how this part of the argument holds up.

A recent study by Peritz, one of the first to exhaustively treat the research literature of librarianship, is of great use here.[10] From this study we learn that the period between 1960 and 1970 saw a significant increase in output, especially for the last five years of the decade. In fact, rates of growth appear higher in library science than in many other fields.[11] Most of the literature centers on university, college, and special libraries, with relatively little work on public and school libraries.[12]

The concerns of special librarianship, as many would suspect, dominate the user studies. Fully half deal with professional patrons, and user studies dealing with a specific subject matter almost always treat subject areas of interest mainly to working professionals, rather than those that might interest general or recreational users. Further, a high proportion of these professional users (70 percent) are in the natural sciences or applied scientific fields derived from them. Thus we would say, in drawing general conclusions about user studies, that the scientifically trained library user is disproportionately represented, and that there is a need for studies of public library use and user behavior, and perhaps also a need for those special library users not in the scientific and technical fields.

Methodologically, empirical approaches predominate. In Peritz's study, "empirical" is defined broadly enough to include historical studies, even if they are not quantitatively oriented. Even so, one has the impression that quantitative methods are solidly represented, historical or otherwise. It may be necessary to point out that the dominance of empirical studies in a body of research literature is the norm rather than the exception, for this is true in virtually every academic and professional discipline, with the exception of certain of the humanities fields. It is true for many reasons, perhaps the most important being that theoretical work is not at all easy to fund in academic and professional circles, but this does not really concern us here. What we need to recognize is that library science is following the normal pattern in emphasizing empirical work in its research literature.

Even so, according to Peritz, the number of theoretical papers is also quite significant.[13] Recent applications of citation analysis show that the median number of citations in library science papers is relatively low in comparison with some fields, except for theoretical papers and works on automation.[14] But, of course, this depends entirely on the comparison: low perhaps in relation to articles in humanities journals, but not significantly different from articles in certain social and behavioral sciences fields or in the natural sciences. Reliance on documentation through citation varies by field, and the literature of library science shows the same variation one would expect in a research literature generally. Also, the use of citation-based measures shows a significant increase in the scholarly characteristics of the literature.[15]

We saw in the previous section empirical findings showing a relatively high degree of practitioner participation in the production of professional literature, indicating perhaps a certain pattern in the division of labor in the creation and maintenance of the knowledge base. Peritz's study confirms this dramatically; it shows that practitioners make substantial contributions. At the same time, however, more recent work shows that library educators produce far out of proportion to their small numbers. These findings are important, for they are part of the empirical background of a descriptive study of the field, and they suggest an overall pattern that is distinctive of librarianship.

At one time library educators contributed relatively little, although there have been substantial increases. It is surprising to find that the rate of contribution to the total was as low as 10 percent in the early years of the century, and no higher than 25 percent as late as 1975.[16] But while in fact library educators produce far out of proportion to their numbers, and this is confirmed by a number of recent studies that point to a "small cohort, large output,"[17] the relationship is so startling that it bears spelling out in detail. While library educators constitute less than 1 percent of the population of authors to library and information science journals, they produce close to 25 percent of the articles.[18] Looked at in this way, the message is not that library educators do not produce enough, but that there are not nearly enough of them to produce more.

Of course, the participation of library educators is only part of the story behind the production of research literature; in fact, academic librarians—partly because of their greater numbers and partly because they work in highly professionalized environments—contribute a larger share of the total number of articles produced. A recent study shows that academic librarians provide just over 30 percent of the total, with library educators second at 25 percent.[19] This means that these two groups together are responsible for over half of the literature. A number of other groups contribute also, including publishers, editors, freelance writers, information brokers, library network officers, public, special, and school librarians—but none of these groups by itself contributes more than 10 percent of the total, and most of them are well below that figure.[20] Clearly the best hope in the current division of labor in the production of research articles lies with library educators and academic librarians.

THE KNOWLEDGE BASE REVISITED: THE IDEAL AND THE REALITY

The problem of the knowledge base has been so central to almost all of the literature on the professions that it is worthwhile to consider it further. Reservations about what passes for knowledge in the professions are commonly found in the literature of the professions generally. Thus while Goode is correct in his judgment that librarianship needs development in this area, it is only fair to point out that this observation has also been made by untold librarians.[21] And it has been made not only about librarianship; after all, what occupational group can claim that its knowledge base needs no further development? What body of knowledge—theoretical or otherwise—has achieved the perfection implied by the notion of complete professionalization?

Beyond this is another dimension that is ignored by many assessments of the knowledge base; that is the "political," to use the term in its loose contemporary sense. We speak, for example, of "office politics," the "politics" of the family, and so on, thinking not of the formal machinery of elections or party affiliations, but rather of the informal power structures that all social activities exhibit. These considerations also affect the intellectual basis of professional work and should be kept in mind when discussing them. Unfortunately, until the relatively recent development of the occupational control approach, these considerations were not widely recognized or addressed, and thus many of the older ideas about professional knowledge are characterized by a striking political naivety. Evaluating knowledge bases is thus not merely a matter of assessing their contents, but also of understanding the interests they reinforce.[22] Much of what passes for knowledge in the professions and in academic life is not always as theoretical or scientific as one might think, and numerous extraneous factors enter into its production and dissemination, some having little or nothing to do with pure inquiry.

A great deal has been made in recent years, for example, of the system of peer review in journal publishing. Papers should be selected, the classic argument goes, only after "blind" review. The critic or referee should not know whose paper he or she is judging; perhaps ideally, the editor should not know it either until after the review is complete. And, of course, peer review in the form of the "double blind referee" system of publication is indeed a very important step in the elimination of editorial bias.[23] Before it was systematically adopted in the research professions, papers tended to reflect editorial views almost exclusively. With the reviewing responsibility distributed more equally in a network of professionals, a step is taken in the control of arbitrariness in scholarly communication. Nonetheless empirical studies find that this system does not prevent bias in certain respects, though it does seem to place limits on editorial power.[24] Thus while the old problem of editorial fiat in library literature is serious, its replacement by the referee system will not automatically guarantee a more scientific body of literature.

The Problem of Theoretical Poverty

The lack of an adequate body of theoretically significant knowledge is, as we have seen, an obstacle to the professional development of an occupation. It is often said that library literature has been dominated by short-run practical concerns, indicating some theoretical weakness. But actually this judgment, however common, is only partly true, and certainly not true if applied to the literature as a whole. At the very least, the evidence examined earlier in this section suggests otherwise. What may be more to the point is that the research that exists is in general underused. It is interesting to note, in any case, that the problem of theoretical underdevelopment is not unique to allegedly underdeveloped occupational groups. This is primarily because, as suggested above, the definition of what counts as research in most fields usually refers to empirical work, and so we find theoretical underdevelopment an endemic condition rather than an occasional aberration. For example, recent examinations of the literature of sociology show strong atheoretical or even antitheoretical tendencies—a turn to short, easily fundable empirical studies rarely well integrated into the knowledge base of the field. In a symposium on sociology journals, no less than four contributors cite the lack of significant theoretical work in the major journals of the field.[25] This does not mean that no theoretical work is being done in sociology, but rather that it is not well represented in the official journals and is done in a fragmentary way, preventing theory from exercising a guiding and integrating force.

These points on the politics of professional knowledge are not raised to discredit the importance of the knowledge base, but to illustrate a point already made: there is always a gap between the ideal and the real, which makes comparisons among groups difficult. In looking at much of the earlier literature on the professions, there is an unmistakable sense of a stacked deck. When we compare the rosy ideal of some groups to the reality of others, the former will always look better. Some groups, to be sure, are more secure socially, and to that extent more powerful than others. But this important social fact may not be reflected in that group's knowledge base. Power and knowledge, though certainly related, are not tied together in any easily predictable fashion. Are the most powerful professional groups the ones with the most highly developed knowledge bases? Even a simple comparison between the research professions and the lucrative pursuits of medicine and law would cast doubt on that idea. Of course, the reason for this is that money does not exhaust power, and there is a great deal to be said in favor of the cultural power of dominant academic disciplines. Knowledge is related to power, but it depends on what kind of power is at stake. And in librarianship, there is a cultural gatekeeping function whose significance, though difficult to measure, is undeniable.

When we look at this overall picture, we see the outlines of a body of literature that is not very different from the research literatures of many other fields. Most fields are afflicted with theoretical poverty, and show an overemphasis on empirical work. Most fields show increases in output over longer periods of time. Most fields show citation patterns that vary by type of approach, with theoretical pieces citing more items. Most fields show a tendency to become more sophisticated—particularly in terms of method and technique—as they develop. And, of course, the political problems of knowledge production, reflected in the concerns of peer review, are well distributed. The only way librarianship seems to differ substantially is in relying more, not less, on the practitioner.

THE USES OF FUNCTIONALISM

We rejected Goode's argument about librarianship because traits or functional characteristics have very limited usefulness in distinguishing professions from occupations. Indeed, we question the attempt to draw a neat distinction between the two for reasons already discussed in some detail. But while we should reject the use of traits or functional characteristics as screening devices, we do need to recognize that the older theories of the professions, particularly the functionalist view, are useful in ways not yet considered. By focusing on lists of attributes, the occupation/profession debate obscures this larger contribution. The uses of functionalism, in other words, have nothing to do with telling us who is professional and who is not. Its more positive contribution is that it placed the study of professional work within the broader context of the social system; and it provides us with some tools for understanding typical problems in acting out the professional role.

The theory of the professions as formulated in the classic period of American sociology was a part of a larger theoretical and historical endeavor, which came to be known as structural-functionalism.[26] One of the more remarkable aspects of structural-functionalism is that it aimed to provide a framework for the study of all social life, not just social interaction or culture or social organization or politics, but everything to do with human society. Thinking along these very broad lines, Talcott Parsons developed, over the course of many years and a number of books, the idea of the social system. One of the major problems of understanding social systems, he and others argued, was in the relationship between social structure and personality. Social structure provides a general framework for social life, and somehow this structure becomes a part of the individual personality and is thus translated into the terms of individual behavior and interaction with others. The key link between the individual personality and the vastness of the structure around it is the idea of social role. By enacting a given role, which is in turn defined by widely-shared social norms, a person participates in the system, and finds him- or herself connected to social networks far distant in space and time. The individual personality is not isolated and idiosyncratic, but integrated into the social structure around it. Thus when we study the personality, we are in a sense studying society. And when we look at social structure and culture, we are looking at patterns that are represented in individual behavior.

But the match is rarely perfect, and no individual completely embodies the norms of the larger system. For this reason structural-functionalism has contributed greatly to our understanding of a whole range of problems centering on the interplay between social structure and the social roles we find embedded in it, particularly where there is a problem of "fit." It has clarified these problems as they relate to the complex limitations that social structure places on an individual's ability to fulfill a diverse set of socially shared expectations—the ability, in short, to enact a role. Thus even if this does not help in distinguishing occupations from professions, it is useful in understanding the relationship between social structure and work. As it happens it is equally useful in many other areas, including the family, participation in voluntary associations, community studies, problems of assimilation and acculturation, and others. Social structure can act in a number of ways to create problems in role enactment and also to provide, in its own way, some solutions to these problems we routinely encounter in fulfilling our obligations.

Two major types of problems of role enactment are discussed here, both dealing with blocks to professional development. The first are external; they come from outside the occupation. Examples are various forms of prejudice or objective limitations on professional development such as late career decision. The second are internal, because they come from within. Our example here is "role strain," or the difficulty of enacting a work role that has incompatible obligations.

External Blocks

Examples of external blocks can be found in the area of mobility. A study by Taylor focuses on mobility defined as change of employer. Greater mobility is linked with activity in national associations, continuing education activity, and the production of research and scholarly literature.[27] Professional activity leads to increased mobility chances, and these in turn bring new occasions for further professional involvement. An important part of this is the multiplication of professional contacts that occurs in moving from one place to another. Even without taking other factors into account, greater frequency of professional contact by itself has important implications for professional behavior.

But mobility is blocked, for example, by various forms of prejudice, such as sexism. Some findings about female librarians raise important questions about the feminization thesis. It is true that women have generally lower mobility chances, and thus tend to show lower levels of professional involvement. But salary and mobility are closely associated for females only; low-mobility males are not penalized for lack of movement. (In other words, mobility is important for everyone, but more important if you are female.) On the other hand, Taylor observes that immobile females tend to be significantly older than mobile colleagues of both sexes, suggesting that we need to account for age separately if we are interested in blocks to professional development in female workers. And despite the fact that males are generally more mobile—just as they are in other occupations—this should not obscure the fact that men who are not mobile show the same tendency toward low involvement seen in women who are not mobile.

Other external barriers, such as late career decision (relatively common in librarianship), sex role, and age, are all rooted in general patterns of social structure and culture, and thus impinge upon us, as it were, from the outside. We do not necessarily create them in our dealings with others, but we encounter them as limits on our ability to act. What these barriers have in common is that they condition and limit role performance externally. Late career decision, for example, is rooted in patterns of social behavior that have little to do with any given occupation, but much to do with the social backgrounds of certain people who find their career choices limited early in life by factors more or less beyond their control. Another factor causing late career decision is the condition of the labor market, which changes considerably over time. Because occupations have histories that merge with the larger stream of social life and are themselves embedded in preexisting networks of norms, values, and social rewards, they naturally reflect in various ways the society that surrounds them.

Internal Block: Role Strain

Another kind of obstacle comes only indirectly from the social structure. Most directly its source is in the fact that certain roles by themselves present problems of enactment; certain roles are more difficult to play than others. This obstacle comes from the formal characteristics of the occupation itself and the roles found in it. It takes the form of incompatible demands made upon the role player. Any social group has explicit and implicit norms of behavior that reflect shared values. Norms and values are supported by enforced obligations defining expected role performance. In discussing roles in a given group, we always distinguish between the actual performance and the role itself, which is a more or less enduring pattern of action. Since these two seldom mesh perfectly, we can learn something important about the adequacy of performance by comparing them.

In the internal block, adequacy of performance is checked by this structurally reinforced incompatibility of obligations; the extreme form is "role strain."[28] Classic examples are found in all major types of social roles, in the family, in work, and in leisure. It is quite common in most professional occupations as in academic librarianship, where there is an inescapable competition between allegiance to librarianship and loyalty to an additional subject area.[29] A similar type of strain probably occurs in other fields of librarianship as well. For example, it is likely to occur in school librarianship, where education is the competitor; in library automation; and also in library management, where many of the attitudes and orientations of general managers at a certain point challenge one's affiliation with the original field.[30] The resulting strain is partly dependent on previous educational background, and can be expected to increase as field commitment outside library science increases. Since educational requirements are in many ways tighter now than in the past, this kind of strain presumably will be with us for some time.

The pressure is highest for the librarian with advanced graduate work in the field outside of librarianship. If one's loyalty to librarianship is very strong, some of the ability to give service to users falls off. If one opts for a subject field as a working scholar, it is unlikely that one will make as many contributions to the professional field. This is a problem inherent in librarianship, with its peculiar tension between metascience and science. In a sense, all librarians are caught between maintaining a knowledge of the concerns of the population served and developing their own sphere of professional knowledge. This imposing barrier may perhaps never be totally removed, for it may be too close to the core of the work. But we should notice that a good deal of this tension has to do with our definition of the division of labor in the field as a whole. If we have a group of scholars maintaining the research literature as a whole, this barrier diminishes considerably in importance. At that point the scholarly contributions of working librarians could only add to the professional development of the field.

There is, however, another way of looking at this situation, and that is to see it not as a problem but as a highly useful challenge that encourages the more ambitious workers to develop simultaneously in more than one direction. This may sound paradoxical: what acts as a barrier to further development at the same time can encourage that development. But paradox is not necessarily contradiction, and there is much sense in this view, for it leads us to see barriers as invitations to jump over them. Sensing the strain of the role, some workers may feel frustrated and withdraw some of their commitment. But others will feel stimulated to reconcile, in their own ways, the incompatible obligations. Functionalism here leads us to the insight that the difficulties librarians experience in this area are not only trials but opportunities that will be appreciated by the more enterprising. And this by itself acts as a device for recruiting the kind of worker who responds positively to challenge.

CONCLUSION

Some writers have proposed ways to deal with role strain. Pauline Wilson, for example, argues for changes in the academic socialization of the library educator.[31] Others urge that doctoral and postdoctoral activity concentrate more exclusively on basic research, moderating the traditional focus on practical problems.[32] From a rather different angle, Paul Wasserman argued several years ago that library associations, to relieve some of the strain felt by the librarian who is trying to reconcile the competing obligations of research and practice, should assume more of the functions of the learned society and fewer of the trade association. This observation seems as fresh today as when originally made.[33] All of these are useful attempts to provide solutions to the strain identified by the functionalist viewpoint.

The attempt to turn the functionalist theory to positive use only opens the door to more positive use of all the basic sociological work on the professions. We can move from the relatively narrow and unproductive concern with using theories of the professions as screening devices to a broader and more useful concern with using a theory as a guide to understanding how a given occupation works, what some of its routine problems are, and how they might be solved. This chapter takes the functionalist theory as an example, but this is only a hint of what might be done. In the following chapter, we broaden the focus even more, looking at the sociology of professions and occupations as a whole, asking how it can provide material for further reflection.

NOTES

1. Those who yearn for absolute truth will not find it here. The attempt to settle the question "once and for all" may be part of the old dream of positivism, which evidently still has some appeal. See Michael Harris, "Dialectic of Defeat: Antinomies in Research in Library and Information Science," *Library Trends* 34, 3 (Winter 1986): 515–31.

2. William J. Goode, "The Librarian: From Occupation to Profession?" *Library*

Quarterly (October 1961): 306–20. Later reprinted in the *American Library Association Bulletin* 61 (May 1967): 544–55, it also appeared as " 'Professions' and 'Nonprofessions,' " *Professionalization*, eds. Howard M. Vollmer and Donald L. Mills (Englewood Cliffs, NJ: Prentice-Hall, 1966).

3. Elizabeth Stone, *Factors in the Professional Development of Librarians* (Metuchen, NJ: Scarecrow Press, 1969), pp. 197ff.

4. Bernard Barber, *Logic and Limits of Trust* (New Brunswick, NJ: Rutgers University Press, 1983).

5. Naturally there was considerable resistance from the traditional fields of learning. For a study of how this operated in a specific instance, see Stephen Murray, "Resistance to Sociology at Berkeley," *Journal of the History of Sociology* 2, 2 (Spring 1980): 61–79.

6. Librarianship, like the earlier versions of the social sciences, was once caught up in the progressive era concern with reform and uplift and espoused an openly moralistic stance toward books and reading. Like sociologists who aimed to improve our lives, many librarians saw their role as encouraging people to read only "the best books." See Wayne A. Wiegand, *The Politics of an Emerging Profession: The American Library Association, 1876–1917* (Westport, CT: Greenwood Press, 1986), pp. 229ff.

7. For example, the biomedical literature has been criticized for shortcomings in the area of data analysis. The rise of biostatistics over the last twenty years is, in part, an attempt to correct these. See Frederick Mosteller, "Evaluation: Requirements for Scientific Proof," *Coping with the Biomedical Literature: A Primer for the Scientist and the Clinician*, ed. Kenneth S. Warren (New York: Praeger, 1981), pp. 103–21.

8. Ronald Rayman and Frank W. Goudy, "Research and Publication Requirements in University Libraries," *College and Research Libraries* 41 (January 1980): 43–48.

9. Paula De Simone Watson, "Publication Activity Among Academic Librarians," *College and Research Libraries* 38 (September 1977): 375–84.

10. Bluma C. Peritz, *Research in Library Science as Reflected in the Core Journals of the Profession: A Quantitative Analysis (1950–1975)*, unpublished Ph.D. dissertation, University of California, Berkeley, 1977. An abbreviated version appeared as "The Methods of Library Science Research: Some Results from a Bibliometric Study," *Library Research* 2 (Fall 1980): 251–68. See also by the same author, "Citation Characteristics in Library Science: Some Further Results from a Bibliometric Study," *Library Research* 3 (Spring 1981): 47–65.

11. Peritz, *Research in Library Science*, pp. 158ff.

12. Ibid., p. 168.

13. Ibid., p. 169; see also Peritz, "Methods of Library Science Research," pp. 252ff.

14. Peritz, *Research in Library Science*, p. 177.

15. Ibid.

16. Ibid., pp. 162, 173.

17. John N. Olsgaard and Jane Kinch Olsgaard, "Authorship in Five Library Periodicals," *College and Research Libraries* 41, 1 (January 1980): 52; Paula D. Watson, "Production of Scholarly Articles by Academic Librarians and Library School Faculty," *College and Research Libraries* 46, 4 (July 1985): 337; and Keith Swigger, "Institutional Affiliations of Authors of Research Articles," *Journal of Education for Librarianship and Information Science* 26, 2 (Fall 1985): 107.

18. Swigger, "Institutional Affiliations of Authors," p. 108.

19. Ibid., p. 107.

20. Ibid.

21. For an example that effectively covers a good deal of retrospective ground, see J. Periam Danton, "The Library Press," *Library Trends* 25 (July 1976): 156ff.

22. Many of the more recent writers on the professions stress this to a greater or lesser degree, but the best single example is Magali Larson, *The Rise of Professionalism: A Sociological Analysis* (Berkeley: University of California Press, 1977).

23. Daniel O'Conner and Phyllis Van Orden, "Getting into Print," *College and Research Libraries* 39 (September 1978): 389–96. For the historical and sociological background of manuscript review and its role in scientific communication, see Harriet Zuckerman and Robert K. Merton, "Patterns of Evaluation in Science: Institutionalisation, Structure, and Functions of the Referee System," *Minerva* 9 (1971): 66–100.

24. Diana Crane, "The Gatekeepers of Science: Some Factors Affecting the Selection of Articles for Scientific Journals," *American Sociologist* 2, 4 (1967): 195–201. This is one of the earlier attempts to do an empirical study of the peer review process in scholarly communication, and it provided data on economics, chemistry, and sociology. One of its more interesting findings is that blind review does not prevent a very small group of scholars, representing a small group of institutions, from dominating the major journals. Thus if peer review prevents editorial bias, it does not appear to prevent prestigious institutional affiliations from influencing the selection of articles. It has been a very influential piece; the reader wanting to pursue more recent work along similar lines is referred to the following: Zuckerman and Merton, "Patterns of Evaluation in Science"; Douglas Peters and Stephen J. Ceci, "Peer Review Practices of Psychological Journals: The Fate of Published Articles, Submitted Again," *Behavioral and Brain Sciences* 5, 2 (1982): 187–95; R. Szreter, "Writings and Writers on Education in British Sociology Periodicals, 1953–1979," *British Journal of the Sociology of Education* 4, 2 (1983): 155–68; William E. Snizek et al., "The Second Process of Peer Review: Some Correlates of Comments Published in the ASR (1947–1979)," *Scientometrics* 4, 6 (1982): 417–30; William E. Snizek et al., "The Effect of Theory Group Association on the Evaluative Content of Book Reviews in Sociology," *American Sociologist* 16, 3 (1981): 185–95; W. B. Lacy and L. Busch, "Guardians of Science: Journals and Journal Editors in the Agricultural Sciences," *Rural Sociology* 47, 3 (1982): 429–48; M. J. Mahoney, "Publication, Politics, and Scientific Progress," *Behavioral and Brain Sciences* 5, 2 (1982): 220–21; S. Zsindely, "Editorial Gatekeeping Patterns in International Science Journals: A New Science Indicator," *Scientometrics* 4, 1 (1982): 57–68; Felix M. Berardo, "The Publication Process: An Editor's Perspective," *Journal of Marriage and the Family* 43, 4 (1981): 771–79; Eugene Garfield, "Refereeing and Peer Review: Opinion and Conjecture on the Effectiveness of Refereeing," *Current Contents* 18, 31 (August 4, 1986): 3–11; Eugene Garfield, "Refereeing and Peer Review: Research on Refereeing and Alternatives to the Present System," *Current Contents* 18, 32 (August 11, 1986): 3–12; Helen M. Hughes, "Peer Review," *American Sociologist* 15, 4 (1980): 186; and Robert L. Helmreich et al., "Making It in Academic Psychology: Demographic and Personality Characteristics of Attainment," *Journal of Personality and Social Psychology* 39, 5 (1980): 896–908.

25. Jerry Gaston, "The Big Three and the Status of Sociology," *Contemporary Sociology* 8 (November 1979): 789–93; Norbert Wiley, "Recent Journal Sociology: The Substitution of Method for Theory," *Contemporary Sociology* 8 (November 1979): 793–99; Everett K. Wilson, "Comments from a Servant of the Scattered Family," *Contem-*

porary Sociology 8 November 1979): 804–8; and Morris Zelditch, "Why Was the *ASR* So Atheoretical?" *Contemporary Sociology* 8 November 1979): 808–13.

26. See among many others, Don Martindale, *The Nature and Types of Sociological Theory* (Boston: Houghton-Mifflin, 1981), pp. 411–14, 437–38, 472–77, 480–95; Francois Bourricauld, *The Sociology of Talcott Parsons*, trans. Arthur Goldhammer (Chicago: University of Chicago Press, 1981); Guy Rocher, *Talcott Parsons and American Sociology* (New York: Barnes and Noble, 1975).

27. Ruth M. Taylor, *External Mobility and Professional Involvement in Librarianship*, unpublished Ph.D. dissertation, Rutgers University, 1973. The data used for this study are no longer current, but they can generally be confirmed and updated by checking some more recent studies, for example, Karen F. Smith et al., "Tenured Librarians in Large University Libraries," *College and Research Libraries* 45, 2 (May 1984): 91–98; Briggs C. Nzotta, "The Literature on Librarians' Careers and Mobility in the U.S.A., the U.K., and Nigeria," *International Library Review* 15,4 (October 1983): 317–34; and Judith S. Braunagel, "Job Mobility of Men and Women Librarians and How It Affects Career Advancement," *American Libraries* 10, 11 (December 1979): 643–47.

28. William J. Goode, "A Theory of Role Strain," *American Sociological Review* 25 (August 1960): 483–96.

29. See James W. Grimm, *The Structural Limits of Professionalization: Academic Librarianship as a Test Case*, unpublished Ph.D. dissertation, University of Illinois, 1970.

30. Ralph Edwards, "The Management of Libraries and the Professional Functions of Librarians," *Library Quarterly* 45 (April 1975): 150ff.

31. Pauline Wilson, "Factors Affecting Research Productivity," *Journal of Education for Librarianship* 20 (Summer 1979): 3–24.

32. Herbert S. White and Karen Momenee, "Impact of the Increase in Library Doctorates," *College and Research Libraries* 39 (May 1978): 212.

33. Paul Wasserman, *The New Librarianship: Challenge for Change* (New York: R. R. Bowker, 1972). Wasserman's point was that the library associations have adopted the function of the trade association—shown in the emphasis on showcasing products from the corporate sector—and have unduly neglected the function of promoting and stimulating research. The annual conference of the Association of College and Research Libraries is clearly a step in this direction, but it is not yet clear how significant the work presented there really is. See Caroline Coughlin and Pamela Snelson, "Searching for Research in ACRL Conference Papers," *Journal of Academic Librarianship* 9, 1 (March 1983): 21–26.

7

Search for a New Model: An Exploration

In previous chapters we discussed three models of professional work, as well as the more general historical, social, and cultural background of the professional occupations, suggesting that there is something to retain from each model. Sociologically, the evidence for the control approach is very strong, and, at the very least, no one can write on the professions today and not come to terms with it. But if scientific judgment favors the control approach, at least until historical conditions are sufficiently altered to warrant the construction of a newer model, our interests are somewhat different. We need to use the sociology of the professions to help us understand our own work, and we need not take sides in sociological debates to do so. That is why we may learn from all the models, even if we recognize that some of them have been left behind by fundamental social changes.

The approach here is more akin to a pragmatic or dialectical theory of knowledge than to a conventional scientific approach to argument. If we were strictly scientific, we would say: "Here are three approaches. Which is best supported by evidence?" But, on pragmatic grounds, we might ask: "How might these three different viewpoints be related or combined, or played off one another for the purpose of understanding our work?" This approach is dialectical because it views truth not as a property of a proposition, but rather as something that emerges from contrast between different points of view.

This affects us in two ways. It enables us to see how the models share certain elements—a central core of usefulness not offered by any of the models by itself. It also enables us to see that each represents something about the professions essential to their explanation and understanding. Probably these two points are related; very likely the commonalities exist because each model sheds some light of its own.

COMMON PRESUPPOSITIONS: FREEDOM AND SERVICE

Differences in approach, then, do not eliminate the core of ideas found in all the variations. Even more striking, however, are the "root ideas," or presuppositions, that do not vary from one theory to the other and are never directly expressed. Narrower concepts that vary among the theories are easy to find. There are elements of what is really trait theory talk, for example, in the functionalist view, and elements of both earlier views exist in the control model. What changes is the arrangement and emphasis. Indeed, from a dialectical point of view, this is precisely what we would expect. What is not nearly so evident is the deeper layer of ideas governing some of these immediate theoretical variations. To borrow from linguistics: the "surface grammar" and type of expression vary so much from one model to the next that one can easily miss the "deep structure" that underlies the differences.

This "deep structure" of ideas common to the models is more a matter of general ideological orientations than specific theoretical views about what a profession is. It is part of the background of the general culture that forms the broader context of work and occupations. To uncover some of this deeper structure is to discover some of the philosophical underpinnings of professionalization. It provides a sense of how the emphases in the different models are related to basic human values. Two of these root ideas are freedom and service, and in a sense they are the fundamental notions of professional life. The ability of the professional worker to serve a given set of needs while maintaining a certain level of independence in the definition of those needs is rooted in the common human problem of maintaining a balance between other-oriented needs and self-oriented needs. Without the idea of service, freedom falls into a form of self-assertion, and without the idea of freedom, the notion of service becomes a form of servility.

Thus freedom and service are complementary. Middle-class people, particularly in advanced industrial societies, look to their work for much more than material gain, and those drawn to collegially controlled forms of work find fulfillment in reconciling freedom and service. In order to serve and do it properly, professionals must have a certain irreducible freedom in defining their goals and organizing their routines. But equally, in order to work freely in a responsible way—to work with the corporate freedom of collegiality that is responsive to client need—professionals must see the service as the limit of their freedom. In this very philosophical sense, contemporary professionalism is the attempt to push the values of liberalism beyond simple individualism, to find a natural kind of obligation that checks absolute freedom without recourse to arbitrary restrictions. As a value, freedom speaks to the urge for individual and corporate control over one's own work. Service, on the other hand, is rooted in the need for values that transcend the narrowness of assertion. There is much that is noble in the impulse to be free, but there is no doubt that freedom is very easy to abuse and often brings domination. Indeed, the history of freedom is one way of looking at the history of servitude, and vice versa. The remarkable thing about the idea of professional service is that it recognizes, at least implicitly, the importance of providing for the needs of someone other than oneself. It looks beyond the ability to control a situation for one's own benefit to the ability to exercise control as a means to a more transcendent goal. With the notion of service comes an orientation to the community, of clients as the essential reason for the work in the first place. And this is, of course, one of the major ideological foundations of professionalism.

Alfred North Whitehead, who has made the rise of the modern professions a part of a general theory of modern culture, argues that while ancient civilizations were based largely on craft modes of production, "modern society is a coordination of professions."[1] The gradual passage from the rule of thumb, trial and error orientation of ancient craft society, begun with the development of modern science in the Renaissance, eventually leads to a form of social organization based on the pursuit of knowledge to be used, in the long run, for human betterment. (Clearly Whitehead here is relying on Francis Bacon and other thinkers of the Renaissance.) But the rise of the professions is only partly a cognitive matter; it also represents the modern attempt to reconcile freedom and discipline, and is thus a contemporary social solution to a perennial moral problem. For Whitehead, the "self-governance" of the occupational group is its guarantee against abuse of its freedom. The freedom is corporate, not individual, and from the start it limits that freedom to a special field of expertise.[2] Thus, while some writers think of professionalism as an ideological cover for domination, Whitehead would argue that the broader sphere of human freedom is excluded from control, and thus professionalism represents a morally progressive trend. It coincides roughly with the decline of absolutism in politics and religion, and with the rise of modern democratic idealism.[3]

VERSIONS OF PROFESSIONAL FREEDOM: AUTONOMY, AUTHORITY, AND CONTROL

There is no doubt, however, that on a more practical level freedom occupies a more commanding spot than service. This may be a reflection of the inherently political character of work or, more darkly, a pessimistic comment on human nature, or perhaps some of both. The idea of service is important, in a way indispensable, and is widely acknowledged. But the ideal of freedom plays a more prominent role in the concepts of professionalism we see in the three models. Perhaps from a moral point of view, this is one of the limitations of the professional outlook; certainly some of professionalism's critics come very close to this view. But for our purposes, freedom is so central that it is important to turn to it here to assess the common core of the models.

Freedom is a large and difficult notion, and yet we all know what it means more or less intuitively. Certainly we know when we haven't got it. Pauline Wilson has observed that discussions of professionalization frequently mix different aspects of freedom in work, perhaps because in some way the different elements of autonomy, authority, and control are usually involved in freedom of action, even if they are not the same. She suggests that "autonomy" has distinct overtones of individual freedom, while "control" is most closely related to the group of colleagues acting as a corporate body.[4] This is a key point, for the very fact that control is vested in the group as a whole, or in some recognized body representing its interests, is itself a form of legitimation, or authorization.

Indeed, this is one of the great problems of the trait approach to the professions. Its notion of individual autonomy is not adequate for understanding the crucial importance of transferring authority from individual practitioners to the group. Wilson's very useful suggestion gives us a clue for linking autonomy with the trait theory, and also some indirect confirmation of the link between control and the occupational control model. More importantly, it also pushes us to try and locate the concept of authority more precisely. Even though the idea of authority is at least implicit in all the approaches to the professions, it would seem most closely related to the functionalist theory, which stresses the problem of social integration through shared values and seeks to explain how many different roles and types of roles come to be coordinated. This rough typology provides a definite link between each model and each aspect of professional freedom.

The term *autonomy* is, of course, often used as a synonym of *freedom*, but the idea of freedom is a more complex notion. The affinity of autonomy with the liberal values of individual achievement brings us very close to the trait theory in a number of ways. The trait theory elaborates a concept of professionalism relying heavily on the patterns of freedom supposedly found in medicine, law, and the Protestant clergy, all professional groups in which the idealized or even romanticized notion of the independent practitioner plays a major role. "Hanging out the shingle" and going into practice on one's own, for doctors, lawyers, engineers, and architects, was considered until fairly recently the paradigmatic form of professional practice. Certainly ministers were situated in the organized church, but they too frequently looked to ruggedly individualistic models of practice to sustain them. And in the development of Protestantism in England, the United States, and elsewhere, the importance of the individual sect, often showing a fierce sense of autonomous independence, very much checked the power of the church as an established institution in any case. This orientation toward individualistic definitions of freedom was so prominent at one stage in the development of professionalism that it became a permanent part of its early ideology. The trait theory's stress on autonomy is a reflection of this early ideology; the professional is the learned analogue of the capitalist entrepreneur.

The idea of authority, as noted in Chapter 4, centers on providing legitimacy for the exercise of power. It thus legitimizes both autonomy and control. "Authoritative" individuals can exercise their freedom "properly," and groups can exercise control over their activities legitimately, if they are viewed as the "authorities." On the other side—the side of acceptance and obedience—authority allows people to conform to certain general norms without loss of dignity, because it permits them to define an exercise of power as legitimate. Part of the reason we are able to do this is because authority involves an appeal to shared values, and the acceptance of the values enables us to see our actions as means to ends that we generally agree with. Values are also made tangible in various ways: through effective leadership, formal and informal learning, and symbolic representations in the print media, visual art, and public spectacle. In professional work, values are shared by practitioners and reinforced through education, the association, the process of developing the knowledge base through research, and by colleague contact. Functionalist theory most clearly articulates the social use of authority to accomplish social control and the integration of the different spheres of social action. Thus the idea of authority, though presupposed in any idea of control, seems most closely related to the functionalist theory of the professions.

All the models recognize the group of colleagues in one way or another, but the occupational control model puts considerably more emphasis on it. The trait theory is too individualistic to do more than recognize the group tangentially; functionalism recognizes that there is a corporate identity to an occupation, but does not focus on how the group actually exercises control over work routines. Thus it is quite right, as Wilson suggests, to see the idea of "control" as essentially group oriented, and thus to be most closely related to the newest approach to the study of the professions. In the occupational control model, practitioners develop a sense of group identity by participating in and thus more or less easily accepting shared standards initially developed in the school and more thoroughly worked out in the associations. The primary focus is neither on individual freedom as such, nor on developing means to ensure compliance with norms that reflect much larger issues of social harmony, but more down to earth. Its focus is mainly on translating professional knowledge and values into shared understandings of how to organize the workplace, divide up the labor, provide short- and long-term rewards, and assure a level of day-to-day cohesiveness. Part of the appeal of the control model is in this ability to explain professionalism as a species of ordinary work. Both the trait theory and functionalism, on the other hand, tend to exalt professionalism as something rare, unique, and special, or, put negatively, to mystify it or idealize it—thus the stress on the "esoteric" knowledge base, the aloof forms of authority, the clannishness of the collegial group. Functionalism goes a step further and attempts to connect professional work with a grand mission in the maintenance of the social order.

Some of these differences are shown in Figure 7–1.

DIVERSE STRENGTHS: TRAIT THEORY

Even looked at by itself, the trait theory has some permanent value to be retained. What stands out especially are the professional associations, the knowledge base, and the service orientation. The professional schools are indirectly emphasized through the knowledge base. Probably this is because the trait theory has the oldest roots and goes back to a time when the knowledge base was

Figure 7–1
Aspects of Freedom in Professional Work

Aspect of Freedom	Main Focus	Model
Autonomy	Individual practitioner	Trait Theory
Authority	Legitmacy	Functionalism
Control	Colleague group	Occupational Control

transmitted by methods quite different from those found in the contemporary professional school. The social recognition dimension that figures as part of the trait theory, although of obvious importance, is too dependent on factors beyond the work situation to be of great use in analyzing an occupation's ability to professionalize. If anything changes only over very long periods of time, surely it is social recognition. Only if our view is a very long one, for example, will we recognize that at one time medicine was a marginally reputable line of work and that the clergy far overshadowed it and other professions. The most we can say is that social recognition is subject to considerable long-term historical variation.

At the same time—and this also contributes to the problem of assessing its importance—with periods of this magnitude, the whole meaning of social recognition naturally changes, right along with the enormous social changes that have occurred over the past few centuries. Thus what might count as recognition in seventeenth-century France or England may mean something quite different in eighteenth-century England or in the twentieth-century United States. The biggest of these changes is that now there are a great many occupational groups striving for recognition. This means, among other things, that there are also specialized clientele groups; the diversification and segmentation of the labor market structures groups of users of services as much as it does the occupations providing them. (Of course, this is true for many different occupations, not just the collegially organized ones considered here.) Thus while almost everyone at one time or other will use the services of a librarian, a doctor, or a lawyer, only a few end users will consult a specialist in collection preservation, a pediatric neurologist, or a maritime insurance attorney. In these much more specialized cases, social recognition comes at least partly from the specialized client group. And this kind of recognition, although obviously important for the survival of the professional group, cannot have the power of a recognition pattern that is widely distributed throughout a homogeneous public.

A similar consideration holds for codes of ethics. Like social recognition, they are obviously important. But professions seem to give them a much lower priority than other traits. Ethics codes are so unevenly diffused through the middle-class occupations that it is difficult to consider them essential to professional work. Perhaps the formal code of ethics is of greater significance in what Reeves calls the structurally professionalized groups, where sanctions have a legal character. In normatively professionalized groups, such as librarianship, formal sanctions governing behavior do not exist in legal form, and thus the need to codify is not as strong. But it is obvious that in the area of intellectual freedom librarianship has a central ethical concern that directly affects the autonomy of the professional and the rights of users. Thus, freedom of access is a central value, but its expression in codified form does not seem particularly important. This is evident in a recent study of the development of the ethics code in the ALA. Throughout the earlier periods, the values of intellectual freedom seem absent from its official statements, and there is a strong strain of authoritarianism in earlier versions of the code stressing organizational loyalty. What we think of as the classic liberal core of professional ethics in the field—intellectual freedom, freedom of access, rights of the reader, and so on—comes much later, and does not appear in ALA statements until 1970 and after. In the 1973, 1975, and 1981 statements, the liberal doctrine figures prominently, but this is many decades later.[5] This could be interpreted to mean that ethics codes are an important neglected source of professional cohesion, a policy implication worth considering.

DIVERSE STRENGTHS: FUNCTIONALISM

Functionalism shares with the trait theory a heavy emphasis on the knowledge base; both stress the intellectual or, more narrowly, the cognitive aspects of professional work. But functionalism is a product of a later historical period, and it reflects this in certain ways. If the trait theory does not stress the school as much as the knowledge that the work is based on, functionalism more than takes up the slack. Its distinctive contribution is the recognition that maintaining and transmitting the knowledge base is the official responsibility of the school and the educators. It is not enough that the knowledge base exists and somehow is passed on. Professional knowledge must be officially recognized and established in a social agency that is itself integrated into the larger society. With the knowledge base, the major institution is education, with professional education playing a narrower role in the total process.

In very early childhood education, to take a different example, the institutional setting is likely to be the family or some substitute. But as growth continues, the complexity and variety of knowledge thought to be essential increase and require a more highly specialized approach. Professionalization continues this trend, requiring more differentiation of educational function. Thus the path that begins for all in the family and that, for many middle-class people, leads to professional schooling, is itself only a small part of the overall process of social action. At each step along the way, key values provide a sense of direction and link the development of the individual to enduring social needs. What functionalists call institutionalization is thus a process of regularizing, formalizing, and establishing a setting with a continuing tradition of adaptation to a variety of social demands. In the professions, it establishes the school as a complex organization with a faculty or a staff, providing a place where a tradition of scholarship is encouraged, along with a sense of common occupational culture composed of shared values and general orientations to work. Just as the purpose of the family is to nurture the young in the earliest phase of life, the purpose of the professional school is to transmit this tradition of scholarship and professional culture to new groups of practitioners.

Naturally this is closely related to the trait theory's stress on the knowledge base, but it has much more general social implications. Where the trait theory tends to view professions as relatively independent groups made up of autonomous individuals, functionalism links groups and individuals to a vast web of interlocking social relationships. The functionalist model complements the trait approach rather well here, because in the latter there is not much sense of a larger social process that gives a broader meaning to professional work. Clearly, however, this process is particularly important for normatively professionalized groups that lack legal mechanisms of control. On the other hand, functionalism does not stress the professional association, one additional reason not to abandon the trait model totally.

DIVERSE STRENGTHS: OCCUPATIONAL CONTROL

The occupational control model seems at first to push aside everything except its own version of power—group control over work routines and general definitions of service—and to elevate it to the status of the unique principle of the professionalization process. But this is only superficially true. We saw from the Reeves study that control reflects and is confirmed by the strength of collective orientations toward tasks and routines. But this in turn involves the standard setting functions of the schools and the associations, especially the national ones. According to this model the social control over knowledge that functionalism attributes to the institutionalization process comes from the schools and the associations together, and is reinforced by shared orientations of working librarians. Thus the occupational control model gives some of the same prominence to associations that is found in the trait model, but really only covertly recognizes the institutionalization process. And this is because it stresses the occupation and its routines, rather than its relation to large social processes. The service orientation is more explicitly analyzed by the control model than by either of the other two, for service is defined as type of control.

This model is interactive, involving the schools, the associations, the practitioners' work routines. Functionalism tends, on the other hand, to see control in much more hierarchical terms: more of a "top down" model, from the educational institution to the professional group and then to the practitioner. Reeves's findings on collective orientations speak strongly for the utility of this interactive part of the occupational control model for the library profession. In the trait model, autonomy is based on the training period and the difficulty of mastering the knowledge base, both matters of prime concern to the individual. In the functionalist model, autonomy is situated in the larger context of authority as expressed by dominant social values: the freedom of the professional is really more an expression of social needs than individual preferences. In the occupational control model, control involves most closely the associations, the schools, and the cohesiveness or strength of shared orientations of practitioners. The knowledge base remains implicit in the school and is not given any special prominence.

The individual contributions of the three models are shown in Figure 7–2.

A COMPOSITE MODEL

Is it possible to blend the three models of professionalization into an integrated composite? The attempt is worth making, for it gives us a sense of further development. Looking at areas of convergence, as shown in Figure 7–3, some items recede in importance while others gain.

The main areas of convergence in the composite model are the schools, the associations, and the relation between schools, associations, and the larger social process of providing established professional services. In other areas, convergence is indirect; the entire area of standards is explicit in the control model, implicit in the other two. The importance of cohesion or strength of shared orientations toward work is recognized directly in the control model, only indirectly if at all in the other two. Thus from the standpoint of a social psychology of occupations, the control model is most directly useful, for it focuses on work, interaction, collegiality, and the climate of the workplace. The knowledge base, so central in the trait model, recedes slightly in the functionalist model, where it is represented by the idea of a period of "cognitive training" in the institutionalized school, and is just recognized in the occupational control model.

Application of the Composite Model

Imperfect though the overlap may be, the composite model helps us to understand not only basic professional functions and specializations, but a range of typical professional issues. Selection and reference are examples of functions already mentioned, and they also serve well here.

The composite model helps us to appreciate differences among basic functions. Selection of materials, for example, is only partly influenced by the curriculum of the professional school, where it is taught but not always as a core item of the knowledge base. This is probably because there is a strong connection be-

Figure 7–2
General Comparison of Models

Model	Primary Aspects	Secondary Aspects	Focus
Trait	Autonomy Knowldge Association School	Ethics Code Recognition	Individual
Functionalist	Authority Cognitive Skill Knowledge School	Associations	Institution Society
Control	Control of routines Standards Cohesion	Knowledge Schools Associations	Group

Figure 7–3
Areas of Convergence

Trait	Functionalist	Control
Autonomy	Authority	Work Routine
Associations	Schools	Application of Standards
Schools	Institutionalization	Cohesion of Group
Knowledge Base		

tween materials selection and expertise that lies outside professional education in librarianship. But materials selection is closely related to the professional association, which produces selection tools such as core lists and standards for collection policy and which provides numerous settings where subject specialists and collection development librarians pool their expertise. In this sense, the knowledge base underlying selection and collection development is more closely connected to the associations than to the schools. Other closely related areas of librarianship, such as collection evaluation, preservation, cooperative collection management, and resource sharing, show a similar pattern. Although not core items of the knowledge base in the professional school, they are represented in association activities.

On the other hand, selection and collection development are closely related to a different part of the model, the part contributed by the occupational control approach. The cohesion of the group and its consistency in applying occupational standards are crucial in maintaining the autonomy of the individual selector. By roughly the same process of reasoning, the related areas of cooperative collections work and resource sharing are similarly related to the patterns of control. Indeed, wherever librarians control selection and subsequent disposition of materials, there is of necessity a relatively high degree of cohesion that supports this. In sensitive or controversial weeding or relocation decisions, for example, this is very evident, but it would be true in any situation where users try to influence the character of the collection. Since most users are best informed about their own needs and tend to ignore larger issues, colleagues provide the support that is needed to address questions of balance.

Reference work shows a different pattern in relation to the composite model. Through its connection with general bibliography, which is a core item in professional school curricula and generally required of library school students, reference has a more direct connection with the knowledge base as transmitted by the school. But not everything in reference depends on knowledge of sources, and so there is also a direct connection with the associations, for there are numerous forums and publications sponsored by the associations that contribute to the theory and practice of other aspects of reference librarianship. The pattern here is variable: some types of knowledge and skill (such as online searching) are at least partly represented in school curricula, but some (such as psychological approaches to dealing with users) may or may not be. The connection between reference work and the control model is more ambiguous. The work of the reference librarian is certainly subject to the variables identified by the control approach, but its concentration on face-to-face interaction with users decreases the overall potential for colleague contact, and is thus not as easy for the occupation to control.

It is equally useful to apply the composite model to specific issues, providing something of a case-oriented approach to the model. One of the main issues in selection and collection management today is the determination of the role of collection policy in selection decisions. At stake are further issues, including the subject background of the selector, needs of users, possibilities of resource sharing, and the overall balance of the collection. Once you have developed a policy for a certain area, how do you use it? It seems clear that the association is more helpful in this than the school, for there is probably no way for the professional school curriculum to anticipate practical problems of this kind. And in fact, the Resources and Technical Services Division of the ALA has been concerned with these kinds of issues for some time, and explores them frequently in its journal *Library Resources and Technical Services*. But in this case the most direct connection appears to be with the occupational control model, for it is in the community of colleagues and in the control of work routines that most questions of policy application are worked out. Where standards developed by the association are in the background, they strengthen the control of the group over the work routine. If the decision were left to a library administrator or to a user, occupational control would be weakened.

There are many issues in reference work that parallel the ones used here for selection. One example is the problem of determining when it is appropriate to use one source rather than another. Another is in the choice of subject headings, key words, or other forms of indexing. Here the situation is somewhat different, for these issues are part of the core of professional school curricula; the beginning librarian learns them immediately. They are issues that deal with the basic content of professional knowledge. Thus in these cases the connection between the professional school and the issue is very direct. And because the broad concern with general bibliography and with classification and indexing ensures a minimal level of knowledge, there is not as much slack to be taken up by the associations or by the work group itself in assuring that the job gets done. Of course, associations do concern themselves with increasing professionals' knowledge in these areas, but the need for them to do so is less critical. For similar reasons, the connection between these examples and the occupational control model is also less direct. In other areas of reference work, however, the issues fall somewhere between the school and the association. In rapidly expanding or changing areas of service, associations are responsible for much of the knowledge transmission function as they provide continuing education that is impossible to provide in an institutional setting.

This chapter began with a plea for a flexible or pragmatic approach to applying the sociology of the professions to librarianship. It is clear that if we were to look only at the trait model or the functionalist model or even the occupational control model, we would narrow our options considerably. In looking for a composite model, even as tentative a composite as identified here, we are able to develop something of a general framework that enables us to make comparisons among functions and issues that may at first have seemed incomparable.

NOTES

1. Mainly in *Adventures of Ideas* (New York: Free Press, 1967), pp. 57–62.

2. Ibid., p. 58.

3. Some of this progressive spirit can also be found in a very idealistic approach to the professions, which seems dated now but is still worth considering: R. H. Tawney, *The Acquisitive Society* (New York: Harcourt, Brace, 1920). For useful contemporary reading, see Thomas Haskell, "Professionalism Versus Capitalism: R. H. Tawney, Emile Durkheim and C. S. Peirce on the Disinterestedness of Professional Communities," *The Authority of Experts: Studies in History and Theory*, ed. Thomas Haskell (Bloomington: Indiana University Press, 1984), pp. 180–225.

4. Pauline Wilson, "Professionalism: Focus on the Basics," speech delivered at the School of Library Science, University of Michigan, March 1985.

5. Jonathan Lindsey and Ann E. Prentice, *Professional Ethics and Librarians* (Phoenix, AZ: Oryx Press, 1985), pp. 39ff., 52ff.

8

Librarianship as an Occupation: Suggestions for Research

THE SOCIOLOGICAL STUDY OF OCCUPATIONS

Looking beyond the composite model of the professions discussed in Chapter 7, there is much in the sociological study of work and occupations, apart from the professionalization issue, of value in understanding librarianship. In this chapter we show some of the directions that research on librarianship as an occupation might take in the future.

Research on occupations and professions is a relatively large field, concentrated mainly in sociology and history, with contributions from other disciplines. Here we focus on the sociological aspects. Sociologists have been studying occupations for a long time, and thus even a passing familiarity with sociological literature would be useful in stimulating research.[1] Aside from the many items on the professions and occupations already cited, the field includes many different work groups with no interest at all in the issue of professionalization. This material is a rich source of clues for further work. For example, the journal *Work and Occupations* (formerly *Sociology of Work and Occupations*) publishes studies dealing with occupations and professions; and a newer journal published in England, *Work, Employment, and Society*, adds another source for current material. Even though we focus mainly on collegially controlled occupations, many useful lessons may be learned in studying almost any kind of work from a sociological point of view.

Broadly speaking, research in this area follows a pattern found in most of the social sciences, falling into two broad types: empirical and theoretical. But these two types break down into so many different subtypes that this simple divison is not particularly useful. Empirical work can be quantitative (meaning collection and analysis of numerical data) or qualitative, where there is systematic observation, description, and analysis of behavior without assigning numerical values to observations. Then again, empirical research, whether quantitative or qualitative, may use any number of methods, ranging from the survey to the controlled experiment to direct observation where the researcher participates directly in the life of the group. Theoretical approaches vary from clarification of concepts through analysis to critical and historical discussions of theories to the actual formulation of usable theories as preparation for empirical investigation. This covers a great deal of ground.

All of these are represented in the study of occupations and professions, and any of them could provide a starting point for investigation of our field. Also in some cases, particularly in some of the more interesting examples of successful research, theory and empirical work are combined in intriguing ways. This tells us that in certain cases we cannot distinguish easily between the theoretical and the empirical aspects of research. Hence what follows does not assume that theory and empirical research are always clearly separated.

THE OCCUPATION AS A SOCIAL SYSTEM

One large category of study is the occupational group as a social system. An occupation has a certain type of social organization, in some ways reflecting the organization of the social milieux around it and in other ways differing from these larger milieux quite markedly. The occupation, in other words, is a society on a small scale, with a role structure, norms, values, and sanctions. As a small world of its own, it has its own social structure. There is, in addition to these structural factors, a complex culture associated with any social group, small or large. Groups have a cultural life of their own, with peculiar ways of thinking, acting, and looking at the world. The concept of culture was originally borrowed from biology, where it refers to a medium of growth and development. Applied to social life, it has this same general meaning without the materialistic assumptions. Human culture is indeed a medium of growth and development, and is one of the means for keeping the group alive from one generation to the next. Its atmosphere, however, is a symbolic rather than a tangible one, a medium of skills, ideas, values, and ways of looking at the world that are transmitted from person to person and from group to group, particularly from the more to the less experienced.

Two examples where this might be applied are the study of the professional school and the professional association as social systems and cultures. For most of us the professional school is a relatively short stop on the way to our first job, but it has a much larger importance. It is a network of roles, expectations, norms, values; it has a history and a traditional role within its parent institution; conflict occurs and consensus is achieved; the world that is only shortly inhabited by the student is the more or less permanent home of the faculty member, the dean, and the support personnel who schedule the classes, do the typing, and arrange for the visiting scholar's lecture. For all these different groups, there are relatively standard ways of entering the situation, which sociologists call patterns of recruitment, and, of course, there are many ways of leaving it. And then there are more or less unusual patterns of entering and leaving. When people enter this world, they adjust their speech, their dress, their demeanor, and, to a certain degree, their way of thinking to fit the situation. In short, their identity reflects their participation. But what precisely is this situation, and how do they adjust, and how is identity affected? What are they like when they come in, and how are they different when they leave?

Into this category of empirical work falls the study of the socialization of the library school student into the professional worlds of the library educator and the practitioner. Of course, the socialization of the educators is also worth studying. What is at stake here is the transformation of the person at one stage of life to another; the undergraduate, with patterned allegiance to peers, certain intellectual interests, and certain aspirations from family and earlier educational background, enters the period of professional training. What happens to the self in the process? The adult is not yet fully formed, the apron strings of early adulthood have not been completely cut, but a choice has been made. How and why is this choice made, and how might that influence the development of the beginner in his or her choice of types of professional training? There has been very little work done on this.[2] Various studies have covered medical students, law students, nurses, graduate students, and other groups, any of which would provide useful clues.[3] Library school students might be studied with survey methods, controlled experiments, direct observation, and indeed in many other ways, just as these other groups have been studied. Pauline Wilson's essay on the library educator has broken the ground and suggested many topics for further research: the reward system of the group, patterns of recruitment, typical configurations of value, group norms among library educators, and a number of others.[4] Clearly the relationship between library educators and the general culture of academia on the one hand, and the culture of the professional group on the other also needs to be studied.

Somewhat different in focus but closely related to socialization studies are studies of the school as a system of social roles and a type of organization with both formal and informal aspects. We can study its communication patterns, the type of management styles found in it (what is sometimes called its "organizational climate"), how decisions are made, and how information flows through it. We can study how things look on paper and how this relates to the way the organization's members perceive it and try to come to some conclusion about how the organization "really works." And, of course, as an organization the library school is, like the library educator, situated in a larger milieu, the organizational and cultural complexity of the large university. This provides an additional set of starting points for further research: how the library school is related to other organized units on the campus (formally, informally, communication patterns, and so on). These kinds of concerns have been raised, usually by the administrators of large libraries, in research about libraries as complex organizations, but they could just as well be raised about library schools.

The professional association is a voluntary organization. We are born into a family or an ethnic or linguistic group, and although we can later choose to reject or abandon such groups, it is usually extremely difficult and costly to do so. Professional organizations, on the other hand, generally reflect conscious choices and mature interests. We join them because we want to or because we feel that it is in our interests to do so. Unlike the older "closed shop" unions of the industrial period, professional associations are voluntary, although, of course, there are costs if we choose to ignore them. As a recognizable organizational type, the association has a role structure, an organizational climate, certain goals and values, patterns of communication and information flow, all of which can be studied as they can be in any organization. Also there are many manageable research questions that can be asked about the role of the association in achieving its purposes. In librarianship, the same types of considerations apply to a number of important specialized associations, such as the Association of College and Research Libraries, the Special Library Association, the Medical Library Association, as well as to the ALA. Of course, there are also student organizations presumably playing some role in the occupation as a whole and bearing some relation to the major associations.

Some specific questions that might be asked about associations in relation to the concerns of collegial occupations are: do they encourage the development of the knowledge base as it is cultivated in the school, or are they more oriented toward the practitioner who has left school? How in general are the associations related to the schools, other than in obvious areas such as accreditation? Are there, for example, informal links between major associations and schools that need to be studied? Do certain people or types of people rotate between top positions in the associations and the schools? Do associations support or represent some definition of professional work? Of professional freedom? Do they support the notion of the autonomy of the individual practitioner, or do they tend more toward the control model's notion of the power of the group? More generally, do the associations, particularly the central ones, tend toward a certain ideology or general way of looking at things?

PROFESSIONAL CULTURE

It is clear that the concept of the occupation as a social system includes both the structural and cultural aspects of the life of the group. But the culture is complex and rich enough that it might become the focus for a type of study in which theoretical and empirical concerns would hold about equal importance and would in any case be closely related. An occupational culture, as we have seen, is a symbolic medium whose main purposes are the transmission of the knowledge, skill, and also the lore and mythology of the group.[5] At a certain point it even produces its own popular culture, complete with heroic figures and anecdotal lore.

In its more concrete dimensions, this group culture becomes visible in the socialization process, in the professional conduct of practitioners, in the activities of the library educator, and, in a distorted form, in public opinion and outside recognition. But it also shades off into the more nebulous realm of shared value and the idea of participation in a common type of basic life activity. Supposing that we developed some fairly clear idea of the social structure of librarianship, what would we be inclined to say about its occupational culture? What are its leading symbols, its primary ceremonies and rituals? What does it mean to "think like a librarian"? To look at the world from the viewpoint of the librarian? Of course, it is difficult to find a convenient label for something at once so amorphous and so complex, and labeling in any case is not what we need as an end product. What we are looking for is a sense of the genius of the group, what Everett Hughes called "the basic moving spirit" of the work.[6]

The Bibliographic Imagination

Sociologist C. Wright Mills summarized for a whole generation of scholars the "basic moving spirit" of sociology by speaking of the "sociological imagination."[7] He defined this as a grasp of the interplay between biography, history, and social structure. The details do not concern us here, but it suggests a similar kind of work that needs to be done in the field of librarianship. We have suggested that the core of librarianship is a three-part interplay among the organizational structure of knowledge, the study of users and patterns of information use, and the values associated with the theory of intellectual freedom. This is one version of the bibliographic imagination. Where the sociologist looks at the typical life courses of individuals and groups (biography) and places them both in the much larger contexts of history and contemporary social structure, the librarian looks at the same individuals and groups mainly as users of information services, placing information needs within the broader contexts of the organization of knowledge and the values of intellectual freedom. Where the sociologist culti- vates a sociological imagination that prevents the study of social life from falling into the triviality of narrow empiricism, the bibliographic imagination unites the routine work of the field with the larger dimensions of the universe of human knowledge and the values of intellectual freedom. Are there other versions of the "basic moving spirit"?

Professional Ideology

The study of a group's culture leads us almost inevitably to the study of its world view as a symbolic system, a combination of ideas, values, prejudices, moral and aesthetic principles, and fundamental philosophical assumptions. This culture can in certain ways be viewed as value-neutral, but the idea of ideology stresses above all the way we become, by virtue of our group membership, committed to a certain way of life as essentially our own, as expressing many of our deepest convictions. An ideology is thus a symbolically expressed system of beliefs. An occupational or professional "ideology" is that aspect of the belief system of the culture that expresses members' views of right and wrong, just and unjust, proper and improper, beautiful and ugly, real and imaginary, and thus the foundation for its shared views of almost all work-related issues. It is inherently normative. While this notion is obviously rooted in a much more general concept of ideology, we are looking here at its occupational form. When we study occupational or professional ideology, we are looking at the fundamental outlook that shapes everything else: the sense of what is important, what counts as a serious problem, what modes of thought dominate discussion, what methods of solving problems are approved, and in general how the work should be carried out.

This topic is heavily theoretical, but it lends itself to empirical investigation.[8] Some years ago, for example, C. Wright Mills devised a relatively simple content analysis technique for studying basic texts and major theoretical statements that revealed the ideological assumptions coloring the development of sociology in the period between the World Wars I and II. Among other things, Mills discovered that many of the sociologists of this period were assuming the values of rural and small town life in a period when the United States was very rapidly urbanizing. And, of course, this could easily be applied to any occupation that has a strong cognitive or intellectual component to its work. In fact something like this has already been done by Paul Wasserman, Mary Lee Bundy, Sanford Berman, Michael Harris, and others, who have in effect been studying the ideology of librarianship if not precisely in those terms. Still there is much more that might be done. Our susceptibility to technocratic liberalism, with its idealization of science, is one very obvious direction that an ideological analysis might take.[9]

We should stop long enough to suggest a framework for research in the area of professional ideology. Dibble identifies a number of areas in which research on occupational ideologies moves from purely theoretical questions to empirical ones: the relation between specific forms of occupational organization and ideological structure, the extent to which an occupation's values are found distributed throughout the general population, the use of the ideology to justify the ways of the group to outsiders, and others. Once some of this work has been done, one could easily imagine some very useful work that incorporated it into the study of occupations and the process of professionalization.[10]

TASK AND FUNCTION STUDIES

The focus shifts here from the occupation as a whole, or a sizeable occupational subtype, to the identification of specific roles or sets of work roles as research problems. This type of research is already relatively common in librarianship, even if it could be better integrated into some of the broader concerns discussed above. In an earlier context we talked about the functionalist project of analyzing types of work roles in terms of role strain. But the focus on the work role in task and function studies is much more specific, and has mainly to do with the practical considerations of job analysis and effectiveness. There are many good examples of research of this kind, almost all falling into the empirical category. Of course, William Reeves's study is a model of this kind, with its isolation of reference and selection as dominant themes for task and function analysis, but there are other task areas, including selection, online searching, and cataloging, that have received some attention.[11]

While librarianship itself is reasonably well mapped in this respect, this is probably not the case for many task areas in closely related occupations such as curatorship, archives management, systems analysis, documentation, information storage and retrieval, media services, information brokering, and library administration. Even a simple descriptive task analysis in many of these cases would be informative, if only because the various groups frequently do not understand very well what the others are about. The larger payoff, however, would lie more in new possibilities for comparison and contrast among the various occupational sectors found in libraries and information centers.

HISTORICAL

With some important exceptions, the whole area of historical research on the occupation, particularly the sociologically informed variety, is one of the major gaps to be filled. There has been a great deal of history written by librarians, but there is still no systematic or comprehensive history of librarianship. There are some useful beginnings, however, covering significant periods in the history of public librarianship.[12] Of course, there have been many histories of libraries and many biographical studies of eminent librarians, and these provide some essential background, but the profession itself, though several centuries old, has yet to find its historian. Thus we have on the one hand a powerful institutional or organizational bias and on the other an individualistic one, which have so far prevented the emergence of a body systematic occupational history.

Some exceptions should be noted, however, for they may be the beginning of a new trend. If part of the history of an occupation is the story of its key associations, we can at least say that we have partial coverage of the ALA, and a full-length study of the Association of American Library Schools.[13] And if another essential part of that history is the story of its professional schools, we should certainly thank John Richardson for carefully documenting the claim that the Graduate Library School at the University of Chicago has "radically altered our profession in several significant ways."[14] In general the historical development of library education is reasonably well covered; it will be interesting to see if this material can be integrated into an occupational history.[15] There should be more historical work of this kind, and more of what produced a lone study of the earliest period of librarianship, illuminating its origins in the oral intellectual culture of ancient Greece.[16] Perhaps something similar could be done for other crucial historical periods.

Chapter 2 noted the feminization thesis and suggested that it could not by itself be used as a means for explaining occupational development. Nonetheless, it remains true that one of the brighter spots in library history is in the area of women in librarianship, for here there is something approaching the kind of creativity and systematic industry required for a serious accumulation of knowledge. Even though this work is more historical than sociological, it shows enough signs of openness to methods from other disciplines to give a sense of how the entire occupation might be treated historically by starting with sex role, gender role, and the notion of feminized intellectual culture.[17] In fact the distinction between the more biologically based concept of sex role, and the more culturally based concept of gender role would be an excellent place to begin. It is important to understand that this body of work is not focusing exclusively on women, but rather on sex and gender as a complex interaction of male and female roles in the historical development of librarianship. In doing so it combines recent social history, the sociology of sex and gender, and the history of librarianship in a promising fashion.

SOCIAL AND DEMOGRAPHIC

Every occupation is situated in a much larger and more complex society, and its members have various backgrounds that in some way affect the way they work. These include social class, early childhood socialization, education of parents, marital status, and sex/gender roles. Some of these have been studied a little, some not at all. Probably none has had the extended treatment required. The study of sex and gender, as we have seen, is off to a good start among the historians, but not much of the voluminous sociological and anthropological work on the subject has been assimilated. Basically, these social and demographic topics suggest empirical questions that can be approached with almost any standard method of data gathering and analysis.[18]

Of the work already done in this area, much of it is generally descriptive and highly useful; it provides a kind of social and demographic survey of the occupation. The findings are useful not only because they describe the occupation's members, but also because they are the basis of comparative studies. More practically, such findings are of obvious value to planners and policymakers, both in the associations and in the schools, because they provide material for estimating the size of the profession, its labor market situation, likely patterns of mobility, and related matters. But while it is obviously important for such work to continue, it would be useful if some of it were more narrowly focused on special problems. There are many ways in which this might be done that would enable us to move beyond general sociological descriptions of the occupation.

In the area of sex roles, for example, there are many hypotheses that have been tested and retested for various population groups, but probably not for librarians, and many of these provide clues for interesting descriptive findings. In the late 1960s, for example, Mattina Horner advanced the "fear of success" hypothesis to explain some achievement differences between women and men.

Despite some strong evidence in its favor, other researchers were unable to replicate the findings and in some cases found evidence against it, probably because the succeeding groups of researchers discovered important differences in sex role identification in different groups. In the 1970s, R. M. Kanter studied differences in male and female managerial styles in corporations.[19] One can easily imagine similar studies of librarians, library administrators, and other related groups that would build on and expand some of the historical work on women in librarianship.

There is another type of social and demographic survey work whose descriptive focus is not on the individual worker but on the relationship between the occupational group as a whole and the world outside it. In this category are studies of the socioeconomic role of the profession, its significance in relation to major social institutions, and its response to socioeconomic, political, cultural, and demographic changes. This type of work has already begun, notably with large-scale surveys of the information treating occupations.[20] It should provide yet another source of empirical data for those studying librarianship as an occupation.

THEORETICAL

It may be too idealistic to hope that theoretical work will be done in addition to the empirical, but there are many more or less purely theoretical topics that should be explored. At this point, almost any kind of theoretical work would be welcome, particularly if it exercises the function of integrating and synthesizing empirical investigations. Indeed, one of the very first theoretical tasks might well be the comparative analysis, classification, and sorting out of theories with an eye toward their usefulness for the study of the occupation. This book is a first step in that direction, but it only opens the door. Thus we might do what is sometimes called "paradigm analysis" to provide a sense of which theoretical perspectives are well represented and which are not. The emerging paradigms might be perspectives already found in librarianship or some from other fields, particularly the social and behavioral sciences, but also from philosophy, literary and cultural criticism, and history.[21]

The sorting out phase then begins to gauge the various theoretical viewpoints in terms of their influence or power within the field, suggests revisions in the paradigms to try and encourage certain directions of research, urges the abandonment of older and less useful perspectives, calls for new ones, and so on. This kind of theoretical analysis has an obvious relevance to and overlaps with the analysis of professional ideology, and that in itself is a fascinating topic. Once we have an analysis that surveys a reasonable number of perspectives, a number of directions are possible. For our purposes the important thing is to use one or more of the paradigms or general orientations as a clue to doing research on the occupation. This might in some cases lead us back to one of our earlier suggestions, or it might point in an entirely new direction.

Conceptual Analysis

A great deal of what counts as theory in scholarly work generally is really a preliminary to using theory to do research, but it is absolutely necessary. Closely related to classifying, sorting, and evaluating theoretical orientations, and just as fundamental to doing useful research, is the conceptual analysis of basic ideas and propositions. This very general intellectual operation is most common in philosophy, where it forms the essence of a certain type of philosophical method. It does not by itself suggest substantive areas, but rather is a kind of general analytical tool for clearing the ground.

One example of how this might work is easily seen in analyzing the difference between a profession and a work organization. This seems obvious, and yet there is widespread confusion between the two analytically distinct spheres. As we have noted many times, almost all of us, professionals or not, work in complex organizations. In addition, our occupations themselves are highly complex organizations. But for a variety of reasons, the most important being the unequal distribution of administrative power, we often collapse the professional context into the organizational one. We act, in other words, as if the profession were reducible to the organization in which the practitioner works. But the occupation is never confined to the four walls of the local organization; and indeed this local organizational context is only the immediate setting for practice. The occupation stretches back in historical time, and spatially it extends over immense geographic areas. Our colleagues include professionals who lived and worked several centuries ago, some just entering and others just leaving the occupation, and colleagues who work everywhere in the world. In this sense the occupation is vastly more important and influential than any organizational setting. Conceptual analysis of this kind is what led Heim and Estabrook to distinguish between "career patterns" (rising in the local hierarchy) and "career stages" (professional development in the broader sense).[22]

To show how this kind of conceptual analysis can bear some immediate fruit, consider how it leads us straight to ideological critique. The tendency to assume that the organization is the fundamental unit of analysis is one of the forces that has blocked the study of the profession and the occupation: it is the administrative ideology at work. Library administrators, really a separate occupational group long since split off from the main occupation, tend to think in terms of the organizations they manage, and since these organizations are often situated within larger organizations, their main focus is elsewhere—the university, the government bureau, boards of supervisors, and other outside forces. The administrator's reference group includes other administrators whose managerial reach extends over a number of occupational groups. Thus it is not at all surprising that administrators assume the primacy of the organization, but this assumption should not be made by librarians or by researchers who are interested in studying the development of librarianship.

Other Theoretical Ideas

Other ideas for theoretical work can be found by looking at the models already examined and filling in some of the more obvious gaps. There is a group of interesting issues surrounding the relation between occupational control, the autonomy of the individual worker, and the degree to which the occupation is situated in a complex set of organizations and institutions. For example, one might ask if the process of "establishing" professional education in the graduate and professional schools has any effect on the kinds of autonomy we find in different work situations. Looking at the work situation more directly, there is much that could be done with the relation between individual autonomy on the one hand and the control mechanisms of the group as a whole. How much of the autonomy that is so stressed in the trait theory, for example, is sacrificed to the group interests that prevail in the control model?

A similar question with a slightly different focus substitutes "cohesion" for control, and then the question arises of the relation between types and levels of group cohesion and individual autonomy. This in turn raises the question of the relation between cohesion and control. Obviously they are related, but how? Intuitively, we would probably argue that cohesion is somehow the foundation of control, for without it the group has no common basis for action. But how is this achieved in librarianship? How do common understandings develop? Presumably this is somehow affected by the educational process and by colleagues. But how? To explore this we would have to understand something of the social psychology of group membership and identification, and then apply it to the occupational setting.

Many questions arise in the interplay of the three models of professionalization, one of the reasons why we did not totally abandon the trait model and maintain an interest in the functionalist model, even though the trend in the sociology of occupations and professions is definitely in the direction of the control model. One such question plays the functionalist view off the control model by asking: "What is the relation between the cohesiveness of groups of professional workers and their student experiences?" Is there something about the experience of professional education that prepares us to be cooperative, group oriented, supportive of group interests—what is it that translates the intellectual experience of the school, in other words, into the terms of collegiality? This involves an attempt to understand how professional education contributes to the formation of the self. And this leads us to some ground already covered in a suggestion for empirical research: professional socialization.

Another highly theoretical question is the study of the knowledge base: its development and recommendations for its growth. This is very clearly related to the paradigm analysis noted above, and, of course, has for some time been a major concern of library educators. But while the knowledge base and its development have long been considered as problems internal to library education, it would be useful to see this kind of work more directly connected with the whole spectrum of occupational and professional issues raised here: professional socialization, the character of the occupational group, professional ideology, the school as a role system, the nature of collegial control, and others.

CONCLUSION

These suggestions may prompt some ideas for future research. Of course, educators and practitioners will continue to do research in cataloging and classification, indexing, formal communication, bibliography, reference work, the behavior of library users, and a number of other central areas. The sociology of occupations provides some complementary perspectives for thinking about librarianship as a form of work that is simultaneously rooted in scholarship and professional practice.

But there is something beyond this, which may be of even greater value— the sociological approach to work is inherently critical and liberating, provided we follow it far enough. Perhaps this is because, as many sociologists have observed, sociology itself is an inherently critical enterprise. It certainly has performed that function here, for it shows a way to avoid some of the blind alleys that narrow views of "professionalism" and "professionalization" can lead to. When we take professionalization models naively, as scorecards to rate occupations, they fail to lead beyond the most obvious sorting devices; and this is not sociology, but rather a form of status seeking. But when we look at the emergence of the occupational control theory of the professions, we begin to see the earlier views as part of a larger pattern. Traits, functions, and forms of control come together in certain occupations, producing and sustaining collegiality.

We make an equally significant step when we realize that the professional occupations can also be studied as occupations *simpliciter*, for this leads us to the sociological study of work as one of the fundamental types of human activity. From parochial applications of the trait theory and functionalism, we come to a more ecumenical sense of collegial control as a basic problem in all professional occupations. And from this we make an even larger step, seeing professional work in the larger context of all kinds of work. Librarians, like teachers, nurses, doctors, lawyers, and engineers, all have basically collegial concerns and certain basic similarities of social and intellectual background. But all of these have something in common with occupations that may not share this background at all—with taxi drivers, circus performers, bank tellers, athletes, longshoremen, and bartenders. And that is simply that they are organized cultures of work, ways of life, with ways of thinking and acting, and distinctive value orientations. They are social worlds, waiting to be explored.

NOTES

1. For an overview of the earlier period, see William H. Form, "Occupations and Careers," *International Encyclopedia of the Social Sciences* (New York: Macmillan, 1968). See also Elliot Krause, *The Sociology of Occupations* (Boston: Little, Brown, 1971); Ronald Pavalko, *The Sociology of Occupations* (Itasca, IL: F. E. Peacock, 1971); and Paul D. Montagna, *Occupations and Society: Toward a Sociology of the Labor Market* (New York: Wiley, 1977).

2. For initial explorations, see Barton T. Clark and Thomas M. Gaughan, "Socialization of Library School Students: A Framework for Analysis of a Current Problem," *Journal of Education for Librarianship* 19 (Spring 1979): 283–93; and Pauline Wilson, "Factors Effecting Research Productivity," *Journal of Education for Librarianship* 20 (Summer 1979): 3–24.

3. Howard S. Becker, *Boys in White: Student Culture in Medical School* (Chicago: University of Chicago Press, 1961); Robert K. Merton et al., *The Student Physician* (Cambridge: Harvard University Press, 1957); Donald Light, "Uncertainty and Control in Professional Training," *Journal of Health and Social Behavior* 20 (December 1979): 310–22; Everett C. Hughes, *The Sociological Eye* (New Brunswick, NJ: Transaction Books, 1984 [1961]), 387–98; Howard S. Becker and James Carper, "The Development of Identification Within an Occupation," *American Journal of Sociology* 61 (1956): 289–98; D. N. Ashton, "The Transition from School to Work: Notes on the Development of Different Frames of Reference in Young Male Workers," *Sociological Review* 21, 1 (1973): 101–25; S. M. Clearfield, "The Professional Self-Image of the Social Worker," *Journal of Education for Social Work* 13, 1 (1977): 23–30; J. Vanmaanen and S. R. Barley, "Occupational Communities: Culture and Control in Organizations," *Research in Organizational Behavior* 6 (1984): 287–365.

4. Pauline Wilson, "Factors Effecting Research Productivity," pp. 3–24.

5. Obviously, Pauline Wilson has broken ground here as well in her study of stereotype, which fits nicely into the lore and mythology component. *Stereotype and Status: Librarians in the United States* (Westport, CT: Greenwood Press, 1982).

6. Everett Hughes, "Education for a Profession," *Library Quarterly* 31 (October 1961): 391.

7. C. Wright Mills, *The Sociological Imagination* (New York: Oxford University Press, 1959).

8. Vernon K. Dibble, "Occupations and Ideologies," *American Journal of Sociology* 68 (September 1962): 229–41. Reprinted in James Curtis and John Petras, eds., *The Sociology of Knowledge: A Reader* (New York: Praeger, 1970).

9. Paul Wasserman, *The New Librarianship: A Challenge for Change* (New York: R. R. Bowker, 1972); Mary Lee Bundy and Paul Wasserman, "Professionalism Reconsidered," *College and Research Libraries* (1968): pp. 5–26; Sanford Berman, *The Joy of Cataloging: Essays, Letters, and Other Explosions* (Phoenix, AZ: Oryx, 1981); Michael Harris, "Dialectic of Defeat: Antinomies in Research in Library and Information Science," *Library Trends* 34, 3 (Winter 1986): 515–31.

10. Dibble, "Occupations and Ideologies," pp. 434–35, 438, 441.

11. J. Periam Danton, "The Subject Specialist in National and University Libraries,"

Libri 17, 1 (1967): 42–58; Ruth Hafter, *Academic Librarians and Cataloging Networks* (Westport, CT: Greenwood Press, 1985); Frederick Messick, "Subject Specialists in Smaller Academic Libraries," *Library Resources and Technical Services* 21 (Fall 1977): 368–74; Brian Nielsen, "Online Searching and the Deprofessionalization of Librarianship," *Online Review* 4 (September 1980): 215–23; Marcia Pankake, "From Book Selection to Collection Management: Continuity and Advance in an Unending Work," *Advances in Librarianship* 13 (1984): 185–210.

12. Dee Garrison, *Apostles of Culture: The Public Librarian and American Society, 1876–1920* (New York: Free Press, 1979). Garrison's book is important because it provides some of the historical background for the study of the culture and ideology of part of the occupation. In examining the "social ideals held by the library leadership," and by noting the emergence of contrasting ideological commitments in the early period of public librarianship, the historian discovers a key turning point: the transition from the genteel aristocratic notion of the library as a place of high seriousness where people get educated to the idea of the library as a place where recreational needs are met (pp. xiv–xv, 9–10). This major ideological shift in public librarianship occurred somewhere between 1900 and 1920. It raises many additional questions about public librarianship in later periods, and, of course, invites us to study the cultural and ideological climate surrounding various other types of librarianship and other information treating occupations.

13. Wayne A. Wiegand, *The Politics of an Emerging Profession: The American Library Association, 1876–1917* (Westport, CT: Greenwood Press, 1986); Peggy Sullivan, *Carl H. Milam and the American Library Association* (New York: H. W. Wilson, 1976); Donald G. Davis, *The Association of American Library Schools, 1915–1968: An Analytical History* (Metuchen, NJ: Scarecrow Press, 1974).

14. *The Spirit of Inquiry: The Graduate Library School at Chicago, 1921–51* (Chicago: American Library Association, 1982).

15. See, for example, L. Houser and Alvin M. Schrader, *The Search for a Scientific Profession: Library Science Education in the U.S. and Canada* (Metuchen, NJ: Scarecrow Press, 1978); C. Edward Carrol, *The Professionalization of Education for Librarianship* (Metuchen, NJ: Scarecrow Press, 1970); Carl M. White, *The Origin of the American Library School* (New York: Scarecrow, 1961); and Charles D. Churchwell, *The Shaping of American Library Education* (Chicago: American Library Association, 1975).

16. H. Curtis Wright, *The Oral Antecedents of Greek Librarianship* (Provo, UT: Brigham Young University Press, 1977).

17. For examples, see Garrison, *Apostles of Culture*; Suzanne Hildenbrand, "Some Theoretical Considerations on Women in Library History," *Journal of Library History, Philosophy, and Comparative Librarianship* 18, 4 (Fall 1983): 382–90; and Barbara Brand, "Librarianship and Other Female-Intensive Professions," *Journal of Library History, Philosophy, and Comparative Librarianship* 18, 4 (Fall 1983): 391–406. See also Mary Niles Maack, "Women Librarians in France: The First Generation," *Journal of Library History, Philosophy, and Comparative Librarianship* 18, 4 (Fall 1983): 407–49; and Kathleen M. Heim, ed., *Women in Librarianship* (New York: Neal-Schuman, 1983).

18. Some earlier studies set examples for further work: Anita Schiller, *Characteristics of Professional Personnel in College and University Libraries* (Washington, DC: U.S. Department of Health, Education, and Welfare, Office of Education, Bureau of Research, 1968); Elizabeth Stone, *Factors Related to the Professional Development of Librarians*

(Metuchen, NJ: Scarecrow Press, 1969). For more recent material, see Leigh Estabrook and Kathleen M. Heim, ''A Profile of ALA Personal Members,'' *American Libraries* 11 (December 1980): 654–59; and Kathleen M. Heim, ''Demographic and Economic Status of Librarians in the Seventies,'' *Advances in Librarianship* 12 (1982): 1–45.

19. For a review of some of this literature and an application to students in law school, see E. R. Robert and M. F. Winter, ''Sex Role and Success in Law School,'' *Journal of Legal Education* 29, 4 (1978): 449–58; R. M. Kanter, *Men and Women of the Corporation* (New York: Basic Books, 1977). For a good recent example of work that combines sex role and demographic analysis, see Betty Jo Irvine, *Sex Segregation in Librarianship: Demographic and Career Patterns of Academic Library Administrators* (Westport, CT: Greenwood Press, 1985).

20. Anthony Debons, et al. *The Information Professions: Survey of an Emerging Field* (New York: Marcel Dekker, 1981).

21. The term *paradigm* is originally from Thomas Kuhn, *The Structure of Scientific Revolutions* (Chicago: University of Chicago Press, 1962). It has been applied to many specialized fields; one useful precedent is George Ritzer, *Sociology: A Multiple Paradigm Science* (Boston: Allyn and Bacon, 1980). An example of theoretical work in librarianship that applies Kuhn's notion to libraries is Don Swanson, ''Libraries and the Growth of Knowledge,'' *Library Quarterly* 50 (January 1980): 112–34. But such analysis sometimes proceeds without direct use of the term *paradigm*, and these are also relevant. See, for example, Michael Harris, ''Dialectic of Defeat'' and Patrick Wilson, *Second Hand Knowledge: An Inquiry into Cognitive Authority* (Westport, CT: Greenwood Press, 1983).

22. Kathleen M. Heim and Leigh S. Estabrook, ''Career Patterns of Librarians,'' *Drexel Library Quarterly* 17, 3 (Summer 1981): 35–51.

Bibliographical Essay

The endnotes to the preceding chapters provide the interested reader with background material. Those who pursue the matter on their own will find that the production of books and articles in this field has become something of a small industry of its own. So although it is not necessary to repeat what the reader has already seen, it may be helpful here to add some brief remarks about this literature.

The literature falls, more or less, into two categories. First, *research literature* deals with professions as social, economic, or historical phenomena. Its prime focus is analysis, clarification, and explanation, and the works found in this category approach professional life as presenting a series of intriguing intellectual questions. The disciplinary focus varies, with sociology and history predominant. Second, *practitioner oriented works* discuss these issues only tangentially—aside from the important exceptions noted below—and move quickly to practical problems. Both of these types of literature have been significant in writing this book, and both are essential for delving further into the subject.

THE RESEARCH LITERATURE

A number of works provide essential historical background: A. M. Carr-Saunders and P. A. Wilson's *The Professions* (London: Cass, 1964 [1933]); W. J. Reader, *Professional Men: The Rise of the Professional Classes in Nineteenth Century England* (London: Weidenfeld and Nicolson, 1966); Robert Wiebe, *The Search for Order, 1877–1920* (New York: Hill and Wang, 1967); Burton Bledstein, *The Culture of Professionalism* (New York: Norton, 1976); Dee Garrison, *Apostles of Culture: The Public Librarian and American Society, 1876–1920* (New York: Free Press, 1979); and Thomas Haskell, ed., *The Authority of Experts: Studies in History and Theory* (Bloomington: Indiana University Press, 1984). These and other works provide a sense of how professions have developed in response to historical forces.

Because sociologists originally led the way in the study of the professions and have made the most central contributions to the newer approaches to the study of occupational control, the list of sociological works is longer. However, the line between good sociology and history is not at all a perfect one, and some of the most important sociological examples incorporate the historical perspective. For example, Theodore Caplow reconstructs the historical development of the occupational classification schemes of the United States government in his *Sociology of Work* (Westport, CT: Greenwood Press, 1978 [1954]), and Magali Larson in *The Rise of Professionalism: A Sociological Analysis* (Berkeley and Los Angeles: University of California Press, 1977) combines Marxist sociology with some density of historical texture. Another example is provided by Dietrich Rueschemeyer's "Professional Autonomy and the Social Control of Expertise" (*The Sociology of the Professions: Doctors, Lawyers, and Others*, ed. Robert Dingwall and Philip Lewis [London: Macmillan, 1983], pp. 38–58). Probably the best example of sociological work on professions that incorporates both historical insight and method is Paul Starr's *The Social Transformation of American Medicine* (New York: Basic Books, 1982).

But the study of professions and occupations cannot be fully appreciated without the conceptual and theoretical complexity of the three basic sociological models of professional work. Sequential history, no matter how carefully documented, is not sufficient; chains of events must be placed in patterns of ideas, which come from several sources. Good examples are found in Harold Wilensky, "The Professionalization of Everyone?" *American Journal of Sociology* 70 (September 1964): 137–58; William J. Goode, "Theoretical Limits of Professionalization," *The Semi-Professions and Their Prospects*, ed. Amitai Etzioni (New York: Free Press, 1969), pp. 266–313; and many works by Eliot Freidson: for a good summation, see *Professional Powers: A Study of the Institutionalization of Formal Knowledge* (Chicago: University of Chicago Press, 1986). Wilensky and Goode mix vestiges of the trait theory with functionalism; Freidson, an early critic of functionalism, is a major proponent of the occupational control approach. Other works on the control approach are *Professions and Power* by Terence Johnson (London: Macmillan, 1977), and those already mentioned by Larson and Rueschemeyer. Of particular significance for the present work is the control-based empirical study of librarianship by William J. Reeves, *Librarians as Professionals: The Occupation's Impact on Library Work Arrangements* (Lexington, MA: Lexington Books, 1980). The central locus for the functionalist theory of the professions, however, is found in Talcott Parsons, *Essays in Sociological Theory: Pure and Applied* (Glencoe, IL: Free Press, 1949); and "Professions," *International Encyclopedia of the Social Sciences* (New York: Macmillan, 1968).

Theoretically informed history provides a richness of detail; but so does the ethnographic branch of occupational sociology. In fact, some of the most interesting studies are in this category; it excels in the description of everyday work routines. Classic examples are found in a reprint collection of Everett Hughes's papers, *The Sociological Eye* (New Brunswick, NJ: Transaction Books, 1984); and in several studies by Howard S. Becker (for example, "The Professional Dance Musician and His Audience," *American Journal of Sociology* 57 [September 1951]: 136–44; and a landmark study co-authored with Blanche Geer, Everett Hughes, and Anselm Strauss, *Boys in White: Student Culture in Medical School* [Chicago: University of Chicago Press, 1961]).

PRACTITIONER LITERATURE

Material written by librarians and library educators about librarianship as a profession shows much variation. Some examples are more research-oriented than others; these have been most useful in this book. Even this smaller subset of practitioner literature shows some variety of its own.

Some, like Mary Lee Bundy and Paul Wasserman's "Professionalism Reconsidered" (*College and Research Libraries* 29, 1 [January 1968]: 5–26), and Paul Wasserman's *The New Librarianship: Challenge for Change* (New York: R. R. Bowker, 1972), describe and analyze mainly in the service of reform. This is also true of Wilfred Lancaster's futuristic scenarios ("Whither Libraries? Wither Libraries?" *College and Research Libraries* 39, 5 [September 1978]: 345–57), although the ideals driving the analysis are extremely different. The cause of a feminist-based reform of librarianship—yet another ideal—is clearly illustrated in some of the historical work. For example, see Barbara Brand's "Librarianship and Other Female-Intensive Professions" (*Journal of Library History* 18 [Fall 1983]: 391–406), Pauline Wilson's *Stereotype and Status: Librarians in the United States* (Westport, CT: Greenwood Press, 1982), and in Kathleen Weibel and Kathleen M. Heim's *The Role of Women in Librarianship, 1876–1976* (Phoenix, AZ: Oryx Press, 1979).

In other cases, historical scholarship or sociological analysis is used for essentially descriptive and analytical purposes. Some examples are H. Curtis Wright, *Oral Antecedents of Greek Librarianship* (Provo, UT: Brigham Young University Press, 1977); Ralph Edwards, "The Management of Libraries and the Professional Functions of Librarians," *Library Quarterly* 45 (April 1975): 150–60; Pauline Wilson, "Factors Affecting Research Productivity," *Journal of Education for Librarianship* 20 (Summer 1979): 3–24; and Patrick Wilson, "Bibliographical R & D," *The Study of Information: Interdisciplinary Messages*, ed. Fritz Machlup and Una Mansfield (New York: Wiley, 1983), pp. 389–97. Brian Nielsen uses sociological themes to discuss problems of professional role and identity ("Online Searching and the Deprofessionalization of Librarianship," *Online Review* 4 [September 1980]: 215–23; and "Technological Change and Professional Identity," *Proceedings: New Information Technologies-New Opportunities* [Urbana-Champaign: University of Illinois Graduate School of Library and Information Science, 1982]: 101–13).

Finally, there is a category of philosophical work that relies on conceptual analysis and the discovery of leading ideas. Patrick Wilson's notion of "cognitive authority,'' for example, parallels and reflects, in certain respects, the twin notions of (structural and normative) occupational authority developed in Chapter 4 (see *Second Hand Knowledge: An Inquiry into Cognitive Authority* [Westport, CT: Greenwood Press, 1983], p. 202, where Wilson suggests that ''epistemological questions are social questions, and social epistemology is the only epistemology''). In any event the centrality of cognitive authority surely brings it close to the ''bibliographic imagination'' and what Everett Hughes calls the ''basic moving spirit'' of the occupation (*The Sociological Eye*, p. 393).

Index

Academic librarians, contributions to research literature, 104
Academic libraries: level of control in, 63–64, 65; specialization in, 68
ALA. *See* American Library Association
American Library Association: Association of College and Research Libraries, 28; and control, 90, 91; and ethics code, 29, 87, 121; history of, 135; Intellectual Freedom Committee, 87; Library History Round Table, 28; Library Research Round Table, 28; and normative authority, 58; and professionalization of librarianship, 17, n.5; Reference and Adult Services Division, 58, 87; Resources and Technical Services Division, 58, 87, 126; as social system, 132; and standard setting, 87–90; as trade association, 28
Anomie, 10, 11, 12
Apprenticeship, 12
Architectural profession, 118
Archives management, 3
Association of American Library Schools, 135
Association of College and Research Libraries, 58, 132
Authority: as control, 57–58; defined, 57; economic basis, 59, 60–62; in functionalist theory, 118, 119; and legitimization of power, 118–19. *See also* Managerial authority; Occupational authority
Automation, 50, 51, 69, 86
Autonomy: defined, 117; in functionalist theory, 47, 123; general zone, 47, 48, 70, 73; individual, 100; and knowledge, 26–28, 48; and liberalism, 118; in librarianship, 48, 70–71; in occupational control theory, 47–48; and rise of professional associations, 28, 29; special zone, 47, 70, 73; in trait theory, 47, 48, 118, 123; and unionization, 74 n.18; versus control, 47

Bacon, Francis, 7, 8, 117
Berman, Sanford, 134
Brown vs. Board of Education, 25
Bundy, Mary Lee, 134
Bureaucracy, 9–10; and occupational control, 52–53; and professions, 13–15, 47; and social control, 10–11
Butler, Pierce, 39

Capitalism, 32, 33, 49, 81
Classification, 5–6, 8, 71
Classification Research Group, 8
Clerical worker, 88–89
Client control: defined, 45; in legal profession, 48; in librarianship, 46, 65; in medical profession, 46, 48; replacing individual autonomy, 100

Clients, interaction with librarian, 65–66
Collegial control: and authority, 58–62;
    and autonomy, 47–48; challenges to,
    52; and confidentiality, 87; defined, 45;
    and freedom and service, 116; in li-
    brarianship, 45–46, 64–68, 70, 84–87;
    in medical profession, 45–46
Comte, Auguste, 2, 101
Composite model of professionalization,
    application in librarianship, 123, 125–
    27
Council on Library Resources, 68, 90
Culture, 130–31; professional, 23, 132–
    34

Darwinism, 42–43
de Solla Price, Derek, 93 n.6
Dibble, Vernon K., 134
Disenchantment, 10–11, 13
Division of labor: and automation in li-
    braries, 51; and increase in knowledge,
    3–4; and need for liberal education, 81;
    as principle of organization, 11; and
    rise of professions, 1, 3; and role
    strain, 109
Durkheim, Emile, 10–11, 13, 101

Education, 3–4, 12–13, 15; liberal, 77–
    78, 81–83; training schools, 22; uni-
    versity, 22. See also Professional
    schools
Encapsulation, 64, 65
Engineering profession, 118
Estabrook, Leigh S., 138
Ethics, code of, 3, 13, 37 n.21; of Amer-
    ican Library Association, 29, 87, 121;
    development of, 29; principles in, 29–
    31; and professional/client relations,
    31; as professional trait, 22–23; in trait
    theory, 86, 121; violations of, 29–30.
    See also specific professions

Factory system, 1
Freedom: as root idea, 115–19; and
    professional work, 27–28, 50, 120
    (fig.)
Freidson, Eliot, 47, 48, 70, 81
Functionalist theory of professionaliza-
tion, 42–45, 53 n.4, 139; and author-
    ity, 118, 119; and autonomy, 47–48;
    comparison with trait and occupational
    control theories, 124 (fig.), 125 (fig.);
    and control, 123; critique of, 44–45,
    46; and definition of occupation and
    profession, 44, 45, 97–98; and group,
    119; history, 42–43; and occupation/
    profession debate, 106–10; of social
    life, 43–44; strengths of, 121–22;
    structural-functionalism, 107; and trait
    theory, 42–43, 43 (fig.)
Functionalist analysis, 134–35

Goode, William J., 15, 98–101, 104, 106
Guild: Contrasted with association, 28; as
    form of occupational control, 44

Hall, Richard, 14
Harris, Michael, 134
Haug, Marie, 50
Heim, Kathleen M., 138
History: and sociology, 93 n.10; and the-
    ories of professionalization, 44–46
Horner, Mattina, 137
Hughes, Everett, 50, 133

Ideology, professional, 133–34
Indexing systems, 5–6
Industrialization: and discipline, 12; and
    freedom, 12–13; and increase in occu-
    pations, 1; and increase in professions,
    1–2; and individualism, 11–12; and so-
    cial change, 1–2, 10–12
Industrial psychology, 2
Information, expansion of, 4–5
Information fields, 2–4, 74 n.7
Information science, 3
Intellectual freedom, 25, 72–73, 74 n.22,
    121
Intellectual organization, 6–7

Job descriptions, 63
Johnson, Terence, 44–45, 46, 49, 52, 53

Kanter, R. M., 137
Kaplan, Abraham, 5, 6–7

Knowledge: commonsense, 4, 18 n.10; structure of, 7, 82

Knowledge base: application of, 24–26; and autonomy, 48, 73; cognitive dimension of, 71–73; as control, 63, 70–71, 73; diffusion of, 4; and division of labor, 3–4; evaluation of, 104–5; formation of, 23–24; and functionalist theory, 121; growth and development of, 93 n.6, 101–2, 104–6; in librarianship, 71–73; normative dimension of, 71–73; in occupational control theory, 123; as power, 26–28, 106; and prestige, 35–36; as professional trait, 23, 101–2; research on, 139–40; and trait theory, 119–21

Knowledge records, organization of, 5–6

Kuhn, Thomas, 93 n.6

Legal authority: as professional trait, 22, 23. See also Occupational authority, structural

Legal profession: and autonomy, 47–48; and ethics codes, 30–31; freedom in, 15, 118; and structural authority, 59–60

Librarians: bibliographic imagination of, 133; contributions to research literature, 98, 101–2; as generalists, 81–83; interaction with clientele, 65–66; numbers of, 74 n.7; as specialists, 68–69, 82–83, 89; versus other information professionals, 24

Librarianship: as applied metascience, 7–9; authority in, 60–62; and automation, 50, 51, 69, 86; autonomy in, 48, 70–71; and bureaucracy, 14; collegial control in, 64–68; deprofessionalization of, 50–53, 69–70, 91; educational qualifications, 77–78, 81–83, 88–89, 95 n.22; ethics code in, 29, 30, 87, 121; feminization of, 34–35, 108, 136; liberal orientation, 33–34, 38 n.24, 86–87; mediated control in, 65, 67–68, 91; and organization of work, 50–52; and philosophy, 8–9; and prestige, 34–35; as profession, 98–102; professional development in, 107–10; professionaliza-

tion of, 14, 17 n.5; professional versus paraprofessional, 51; and progressive era, 111 n.6; quantitative and analytical ability in, 85–86; research literature, 102–4; rise of modern, 3–4; service background, 33–34; verbal skills in, 84–85

Librarianship, controlling factors in: culture of inquiry, 77–78, 83–84; liberal education background, 77–78, 81–83; maintenance of culture, 77, 78–81

Librarianship, research on: culture of, 132–34; historical, 135–36, 142 n.12; social and demographic, 136–37; as a social system, 130–32; sociological, 129–30; task and function studies, 134–35; theoretical, 26, 137–40

Library: administration of, 50–53; future of, 78–79; history of, 78; importance of, 80. See also specific type of library

Library administrators, 50, 138–39

Library assistant, 88–89

Library educators, contribution to research literature, 103–4

Library Resources and Technical Services, 126

Licensing, 3, 13, 22

Literature, 5–6; growth of, 93 n.6

Managerial authority, 57, 68

Market status, and professionalization, 49, 59–60, 61, 81

Marxist theory of professionalization, 49, 55 n.26; and deprofessionalization, 51

Master of Library Science, 88–90, 91

Materials selection: collegial control in, 67–68; and composite model of professionalization, 123, 125, 126; and occupational control model, 125

Mediated control: and autonomy, 47–48; defined, 45; and deprofessionalization, 52, 69–70; in legal profession, 46; in librarianship, 46, 65, 67–68; replacing individual autonomy, 100

Medical Library Association, 59, 132, 95 n.22

Medical profession: and autonomy, 47–48; and ethics code, 31; freedom in,

15, 118; prestige in, 120; and structural authority, 59–60

Metascience: defined, 7; in information fields, 5–6; librarianship as, 7–9; in linguistics, 7; in mathematics, 7; nature of, 6–7; in philosophy, 7; semiotics, 18 n.13; structuralism, 18 n.13; systems theory, 18 n.13

Mills, C. Wright, 133, 134

Ministry, profession of: ethics codes, 29; freedom of, 15, 118; prestige of, 120; and professional associations, 28

Mobility, and professional development, 108

Molière, 28

Moynihan Report, 25

Natural sciences: and application of pure knowledge, 25; and social change, 1–2

Nielson, Brian, 51–52

Occupation(s): ranking in trait theory, 40; as social system, 97–98; sociological research on, 129–30; versus profession, 44, 47, 97–98

Occupational authority: interaction of normative and structural, 60–62, 61 (fig.), 87, 99–100; normative, 58–59, 91, 121; structural, 59–60, 91, 121

Occupational control theory of professionalization, 44–47, 55 n.32, 139; and autonomy, 47–48, 50; and bureaucracy, 52–53; compared to trait and functionalist theories, 124 (fig.), 125 (fig.); formalization and differentiation, 90–91; and group, 119; and librarianship, 57–62; measurement in, 62–64; and specialization, 68–70; strengths of, 122–23. See also Client control; Collegial control; Marxist theory; Mediated control

Occupational structure, 1; and growth of knowledge base, 3–4

Online searching, 51–52, 66, 93–94 n.11

Ortega y Gasset, José, 9, 80

Pankake, Marcia, 142 n.11

Paraprofessionals, 88–89

Parsons, Talcott, 42, 107

Peer review, 105, 112 n.24

Peritz, Bluma C., 102–4

Personality: and social role, 107; and social structure, 107

Philosophy: and application of pure knowledge, 24; and librarianship, 8–9; as metascience, 7

Plato, 79–80

Practitioners: contributions to research literature, 101–2, 111 n.7; and control theory, 122–23

Prestige, 120; and functionalist theory, 47; and trait theory, 34–36, 47

Printing press, 4–5

Profession(s): and class conflict, 15–16; as control, 44–45; defined, 41–42, 44, 98; ideology, 133–34; increase during industrialization, 1; university connection, 2; versus occupation, 44–45, 47, 97–98; versus work organization, 138

Professional associations, 3, 13; and autonomy of profession, 28, 29; and collegial control, 66; and composite model, 123; and control theory, 122; and ethics codes, 29; and functionalist theory, 122; history of, 28–29; importance of, 62, 65; and materials selection, 125; as professional trait, 22, 23; and reference work, 126, 127; as social systems, 130, 132; as source of normative authority, 58–59; standard setting function, 77–78, 87–90; and trait theory, 119–21; versus learned society, 29, 113 n.33. See also names of specific associations

Professional development: external blocks, 108; internal blocks, 109–10

Professionalization: and acquisition of knowledge base, 23; deprofessionalization, 49–53, 69–70; economic viability of, 81; as response to bureaucracy, 12–15; as response to industrialization, 12–13. See also Composite model; Functionalist theory; Occupational control theory; Trait theory

Professionals, professionalism: autonomy of, 22–23, 26–28, 29, 37 n.14, 47, 50;

encapsulation, 64–65; institutionalization of, 36, 54 n.11; political activism
of, 22; service orientation, 2, 13, 32–
33; theoretical presuppositions, 115–
17; versus amateur, 221

Professional schools: and collegial control, 66, 70; and composite model,
123; and control theory, 122–23; and
functionalist theory, 121–22; identity
forming function, 77–78, 84–87; importance of, 62, 65; knowledge transmitting function, 77–78; as
professional trait, 22–23; and reference
work, 125–26; as social systems, 130–
31; as source or normative authority,
58

Public libraries: collegial control in, 64–
65; level of control in, 63

Reeves, William J., 60–70, 81, 89, 92,
99, 121–23, 135

Reference work: as collegial control, 65–
66; and composite model, 125; and occupational control theory, 126

Research, theoretical versus empirical,
103, 105–6

Richardson, John, 135

Role strain, 109–10

Russell, Bertrand, 7, 8

Saint-Simon, Count Henri de, 2

School libraries, level of control in, 64,
65

Schopenhauer, Arthur, 79–80, 82

Scientific management, 2, 5

Scientific method, 72–73

Service: and capitalism, 32–33; and control theory, 122; definition of, 31, 32;
growth of, 12–13, 32; and librarianship, 33; and professionalization, 2,
12, 32–33, 115–17; and trait theory,
31–34, 119–21

Small, Albion, 101

Snow, C. P., 86

Social change, 1–2

Social classes, and professions, 15–16,
19–20 n.29

Social control, maintenance of, 10

Social recognition. See Prestige

Social role, 107; as block to professional
development, 107–10; enactment, 107–
8

Social sciences: and application of pure
knowledge, 25; and social change, 2

Social structure: and industrialization, 2;
and personality, 107; and social role,
107; and work, 107

Social systems, 107

Social welfare administration, 2

Society: and expansion of information, 4–
5; response to modernization, 10–12

Sociological research: empirical, 129; on
occupations, 129–30; theoretical, 129,
137–40

Sociology, and history, 93 n.10

Sociology of Work and Occupations, 129

Specialization: and industrialization, 9;
and liberal education, 81–83; and occupational control theory, 68–70

Special libraries, level of control in, 63,
65, 67

Special Libraries Association, 59, 132

Spencer, Herbert, 2, 101

Stone, Elizabeth, 98, 102

Structural-functionalism, 107

Task analysis, 134–35

Taylor, Robert S., 84

Taylor, Ruth M., 108

Thomas, W. I., 101

Trait theory of professionalization: and
autonomy, 47–48, 118, 123; characteristics of professions, 22–23; comparison with functionalist and occupational
control theories, 124 (fig.), 125 (fig.);
defined, 21; and definition of occupation and profession, 44, 45, 97–98;
and ethics codes, 86; flaws of, 39–42,
44–45, 46; and full professionalization,
21; and functionalist theory, 42–43, 43
(fig.); and group, 119; in librarianship,
39, 106; measurement of traits, 40;
natural history variant, 39; and prestige, 120; pure trait versus natural history, 21–22; as response to
industrialization, 16; sequence of ac-

quisition, 22–23; strengths of, 119–21; trait interdependence, 35–36. *See also specific professional traits*

Unionization, 44; and autonomy, 74 n.18

Wasserman, Paul, 110, 134
Weber, Max, 10–12, 101
Whitehead, Alfred North, 8, 117
Williamson Report of 1923, 88
Wilson, Patrick, 4, 6, 26

Wilson, Pauline, 64, 65, 110, 117–18, 119, 131
Work, Employment, and Society, 129
Work and Occupations, 129
Workplace: and collegial control, 66, 70–71; and occupational control in librarianship, 62–64; organization of, 138; as source of normative authority, 59

Yeats, William Butler, 11

About the Author

MICHAEL F. WINTER is currently Behavioral Sciences Librarian at the University of California, Davis. He has written *The Professionalization of Librarianship*, and his articles have appeared in the *Journal of Legal Education*, and the *Berkeley Journal of Sociology*.